The Road Almost Taken

The Early Movie Industry
in Fremont, California

Against a Vivid Backdrop
OF THE
American Cultural Scene

Donald Burton Parkhurst

Copyright © 2018 by Donald Burton Parkhurst. All rights reserved.

Edited by Nancy LaFever

Contributions by Helen Gwendolyn Parkhurst-Gerhard and Martin Parkhurst

All sketches by Donald B. Parkhurst

All photos with permission or original

This book or any portion thereof may not be reproduced or used in any manner whatsoever without the express written permission of the publisher except for the use of brief quotations in a scholarly work or book review. For permissions or further information contact Braughler Books LLC at:

   info@braughlerbooks.com

Printed in the United States of America
Published by Braughler Books LLC., Springboro, Ohio

First printing, 2019

ISBN: 978-1-970063-04-2

Library of Congress Control Number: 2018967336

Ordering information: Special discounts are available on quantity purchases by bookstores, corporations, associations, and others. For details, contact the publisher at:

   sales@braughlerbooks.com
   or at 937-58-BOOKS

For questions or comments about this book, please write to:

   info@braughlerbooks.com

Dedication

To my five children, Martin, Helen, Daniel, Gordon, and Karen, and to my dear late wife Naber, whom I pray to see again one day.

Contents

Preface ix
Acknowledgements. 1
About the Book 5
About the Author. 7
Chapter 1: Edison's Influence 9
Chapter 2: From the East Coast to the West Coast. 13
Chapter 3: Gilbert Anderson (AKA Bronco Billy) 19
Chapter 4: S&A Becomes Essanay. 27
Chapter 5: Impact of the of Sherman Antitrust Act 31
Chapter 6: Broncho Billy Prevails. 37
Chapter 7: Westward Migration 39
Chapter 8: Long Term Relationship with Niles Begins 45
Chapter 9: Industrial Age Hardships 49
Chapter 10: Settling into Niles 55
Chapter 11: Enter Charlie Chaplin 61
Chapter 12: Chaos in the Streets. 67
Chapter 13: The Tramp, and the Road Never Taken 71
Chapter 14: A Vivid American Cultural Scene 77
Chapter 15: Trouble Brews as Niles Becomes a Boomtown 83
Chapter 16: That's Show Biz. 87
Chapter 17: Curtain Call 93
Interviews with Fremont Residents. 97
Bibliography. 99

Preface

This book was originally written for California State University as a research project during my master's program. It was recognized by the school as an original contribution and worthy of publication. It has since been sought after and printed by many newspapers and magazines, therefore putting the research into book form for comprehensive public availability seems only logical.

A dual theme runs through this motion picture history, encapsulated in the subtitle: "Against a Vivid Backdrop of the American Cultural Scene." Thus, the narrative alternates from a general description of the country in the early twentieth century to a more specific focus upon the Essanay motion picture studio in Fremont (then called Niles), California. The general provides support and background for the specific. The story of the movie studio frequently broadens into a commentary of larger issues.

Thomas Edison is introduced early on as an important figure, reappearing now and again, his influence hovering over the powerful cartel which he created as a financial venture, and of which the Essanay Company was a charter member. These pages attempt to make it clear that his Motion Picture Patents Company was the inventor's effort toward administrative and financial control of the budding movie industry. This legalistic dimension looms larger as the story progresses.

The central character is an American actor, writer, film director and film producer known as Broncho Billy Anderson, the first American cowboy movie star who founded Essanay Studios. His life and career are traced from boyhood until his death in 1971. There were four aspects of that career: 1) his relationship to his crew of actors and actresses, 2) his business partnership with George Spoor with its ups and downs, increasingly soured by tactical disagreements over the management of Essanay, 3) troubles with the Taft administration as the government closed in to enforce the Sherman anti-trust law, and 4) Anderson's relation to the townspeople of Fremont as the studio moved in to overturn the business and social existence of the place.

The unlikely combination of a modern movie studio with an old-fashioned village was accompanied by quasi-romantic overtones as matters went from a problematic beginning into luxuriant bloom. The town and the industry adapted very well to each other and with mutual profit. Contemporary newspaper accounts added to the testimony of elderly residents justify a tugging at the reader's heartstrings, and this writer takes advantage of that approach. The subplot, however, of the "country maid" and the "city slicker" could have but one outcome, and it is described here in nostalgic terms, especially in the final pages.

Broncho Billy and the Western studio matured together, and these pages describe that maturation as Anderson evolved into a writer, director and star, overseeing at the same time the comedies and dramas being filmed as he was shooting cowboy scenes. The Western film in fact was among the landmark contributions of the Fremont studio and was turned out by the hundreds. A few of them are outlined here, with stress given to their high moral tone. That Anderson intended to teach virtue to young viewers is among the prominent aspects of all his work. The effect of this upon the profession for the ensuing fifty years is described as among the lasting results of the Broncho Billy films.

Considerable space is given to the real-life comedy of off-duty actors who enlivened things in an otherwise sleepy village. Many vignettes featuring Ben Turpin, Wallace Beery, Charlie Chaplin and a host of others were contributed to this study by old-time residents who personally witnessed what they describe. Much of this is new material, never published, for these senior citizens were never interviewed until they sat down with this writer. What they have to say, especially concerning Chaplin, is revealing.

Because of Chaplin's lasting popularity several pages are devoted to the time he spent with Essanay, particularly from the viewpoint of the

Fremont residents who knew him as a neighbor. Those who spoke are unanimous in their opinions, which are recorded here.

At first alluded to, Chaplin is given more serious treatment onward. His relationship with the townspeople, which found him aloof and more or less unapproachable, is given few paragraphs. A comparison of Chaplin with Ben Turpin, a comedian who was with him on the same studio lot, is an important analysis. Few people realize that Chaplin was one of many young actors nurtured by the Fremont studio where he turned out several films including "*The Tramp*." This book calls attention to the virtual blank in every extant author as they skip almost completely Chaplin's vital experience at Anderson's studio. There is a reason for their silence and this author explores it.

The relationship of the town with the studio arrives at a climax. The rosy future anticipated by the city fathers as various industries (attracted to Fremont by the success of Essanay) began to relocate there is contrasted with the hopeless predicament of the studio, which was on the verge of dissolution. Without a word of warning, residents awoke one day to find Broncho Billy and his camera crews gone. The impact of this upon the towns-people is given in some detail.

The story then relaxes into speculation with a discussion of what both San Francisco and Los Angeles would possibly be like today if the movie industry had, in fact, taken firmer hold in northern California where it had enjoyed such an auspicious beginning.

The final paragraphs, in solemn spirit, trail off into a whisper.

—Donald Burton Parkhurst

Acknowledgements

A special thanks to my children who have assisted me in getting this book to publication.

Thanks also to the personal testimonies of senior citizens living in the Niles district of Fremont California with sharp memories of those early years. This book is enlivened by many an unpublished personal vignette of such well-known movie personalities as Charlie Chaplin, Wallace Beery, Ben Turpin, Broncho Billy Anderson and others. The elderly folk, quite young in 1912, who related these tales to me (which I properly cross-checked) are no longer available to any researcher for they have by now all gone to their reward. Previous writers on motion picture history failed to exploit those personal experiences and therefore missed an opportunity to throw a light into this dark corner.

This book therefore stands alone, unique in the field of movie history.

—Donald B. Parkhurst

Previous Publications and Speeches (not inclusive)

1. *The Pacific Historian,* cover article Broncho Billy and Niles California: A Romance of the Early Movies. Volume 26 No. 4. Winter 1982
2. Speech for annual Broncho Billy silent film festival and symposium June 1999 in Niles for the Niles Essanay Preservation Committee. "You, as a person with knowledge of this important and colorful period in the history of Niles, are critical to our project. We need speakers with your expertise and knowledge of Niles events and people to bring the Essanay days to life again." By Irene Vincent-Perez, Vice Chairperson

3. Four-part series on Niles in *The Argus* newspaper December 1970, chronicling the history of the movie industry in Niles, California.
4. Numerous newspapers and magazine articles including *Hayward Review* and the *Fremont Argus, Vallejo Independent Press*, as a cover article for the *Oakland Tribune* with a full page spread on several successive days.
5. From the *Limelight, truth and if possible, a little dignity*. Publication of the Charlie Chaplin film company, A society of Chaplin Enthusiasts. Parkhurst's story was printed in Volume V No. 1 Spring 1999.
6. Editing of *Searching Survivor and the Answer I found*, by Marion Baumann-Parkhurst. A chronicle of Donald Parkhurst's wife as she survived the German concentration camps and found God.
7. WHO'S WHO in California Historical Society 1981, proclaimed as an illustrious biographee in recognition of exceptional achievement, leadership and service as renowned citizen of the Golden State.
8. Cartoon strip "The Yolks on Us" and others. A weekly newspaper cartoon strip, and author of many political cartoons.
9. Speeches to many interest groups

Critical Acclaims and Reviews

"Niles is such a unique place and has such a storied past. I am glad that Don Parkhurst has taken the time to chronicle the early movie history of Niles. Great job Don!"

—Bill Harrison, Mayor of Fremont, CA 2012-2016

Prestigious Nomination for the Ray Billington award in Western History by the editor of *The Pacific Historian* magazine John Porter Bloom, seconded by the history staffs at California State University and Florida State University. Although I did not win the award, the fact I was nominated has marketable significance.

ACKNOWLEDGEMENTS

We think this well-written, generously-illustrated essay fulfills eminently the criteria for the Billington award. It combines a light touch, using appropriate imagery, with sound, exhaustive research. It involves movie "greats" such as Charlie Chaplin and Broncho Billy. It gives a new dimension to our awareness of the westward movement of the motion picture industry, showing very clearly that the latter did not merely plop down into Hollywood or Southern California without exploration and important involvements elsewhere.

—John Porter Bloom, Editor of *The Pacific Historian*

"I've had the bloodhounds out looking for Mr. Parkhurst to thank him for his work and to find out more about him and his research…I was intrigued to see how Parkhurst evoked the mood of the times and set the stage to better understand how strange this Wild West town must have been to the young Charlie Chaplin from the mean streets of London in 1915.

—Editor-In Chief of *Limelight,* Bonnie McCourt.

Congratulations on the publication of your Niles paper in the Argus (newspaper). Your paper was excellent and deserves publication and preservation. It was difficult to do because of scarce resources, and other problems which had plagued early writers on the subject. Your success at overcoming these hurdles and writing a serious, not antiquarian, history of the local movie industry is the major strength of this paper. You should be proud of the accomplishment.

—Richard J. Ursi, Associate Professor of History,
California State University, Hayward, California

About the Book

This book is a true historical account, written in a lively fashion, describing the four-year period in the history of the motion picture industry when it was debuting for a permanent location in, of all places, Fremont, in northern California between San Francisco and San Jose. No historian has ever thrown a light into this darkened corner, meaning that this book is an original contribution to the field. It was during the years 1912-1916, that the Essanay Motion Picture Company was located in the village of Niles (today district of Fremont, California). It was an abortive attempt by the young movie industry to sink its roots in northern California, as preferable to Hollywood. The cowboy had replaced the pioneer as a national hero. You may remember Broncho Billy Anderson and his pioneering Western films and of course Charlie Chaplin and the several movies that he produced there, especially *The Tramp*. This era came to a close so rapidly that the nation never reaped a proper harvest of tradition, literature, or even folk songs, for now it is just a blur on the pages of history. All of this happened but yesterday, so to speak. The dust was thick and undisturbed over those four fascinating years until I got to it. The data I unearthed is firsthand, and the story itself is really neat.

The Niles (now Fremont) movie industry was not only important, but that its demise was a major turning point in the economic, film, and probably political, history of the state.

—Donald B. Parkhurst

About the Author

Donald Burton Parkhurst, a true student of the world, maintains a wide range of interests and is a prolific reader, writer, and loves teaching. He studied theology, history and archaeology, and received his master's degree in history from California State University Hayward, California. While in the Middle East studying archaeology, he excavated a dig for field experience at Jericho with the University of Jerusalem and traveled widely from the Golan Heights to Eilat. While in Israel, he lived with a Jewish family becoming life-long friends. While immersed in their culture and collecting artifacts, he collected material for a book on Mohammed. He experienced bomb blasts, encephalitis, meningitis and skin cancer. What more could a person want? This was followed by riding on top of a railroad car from Egypt (where he taught school near Cairo) crossing the Sahara into the Sudan as far south as Juba for research, nearly dying from dehydration.

In his earlier years he had served in the army during the Korean war. He worked as a hospital laboratory technologist. He became active as an artist and cartoonist, publishing his own material in various newspapers and collaborating with other cartoonists, such as Charles Schultz and Lyman Young. Don's weekly comic strip the "Yolk's on Us" which was especially a big hit. He published many political cartoons that kept up with current events.

He taught art, history and English at the high school and college level. Later "Parky" was instrumental in helping his late wife Marion

Baumann-Parkhurst whom he lovingly referred to as Naber, publish her book on how she survived the German prison camps of WWII and found God (*Searching Survivor and the Answer I Found,* can be found on Amazon).

I

Edison's Influence

A myriad of books has been written on motion picture history, and yet this is a story that has never been told. Competent researchers have devoted little or no attention to this darkened niche of twentieth-century Americana, for scholarly eyes focus upon Southern California for motion picture lore. It is there and nowhere else, we are informed, except in Thomas Edison's ancient laboratory back East, that one will find the beginnings of moviedom, so historians duly converge upon Hollywood's superabundant records when the urge to write comes upon them.

So goes the reasoning. But it rings hollow when we understand two things: 1) that marvelous advances in cameras and projectors were taking place in Europe, especially in France, at the very time the Wizard of Menlo Park was himself churning out camera inventions in series, hedging himself with patents likewise in series, and keenly aware of competition from both sides of the Atlantic. And 2) it holds no water when we realize that it was in California-to-the-*north*, in a backwater village later called Fremont and down the road a piece from Oakland, that a well-heeled movie outfit by the name of Essanay, and with Thomas Edison's imprimatur, was sending down particularly strong roots.

In the first decade or two of the twentieth century, Edison himself, chief among a litany of inventors of the camera, was vaguely aware that of all his brain children, with *this* little jewel, which he called a kinetoscope, he could bequeath his most precious legacy of inventions capped by this revolutionary device known to us as the motion picture camera. As surely as with his light bulb, this unpredictable creation had within itself a sky's-the-limit potential, and proved able to generate a host of new and colorful professions. The discovery of California's gold in 1848, although it quickly propelled the American economy forward, was a minor event when compared with the social upheavals and financial power resulting from the movie industry. The essential difference between them is that the gold mines became barren within a decade or two, whereas the manifold wealth and influence generated by the camera, although it took a little more time, maintained an ever-ascending curve.

Edison's vision for motion pictures was as high-minded as it was legacy conscious, for it was also his intention to forestall Eastern capitalists, who had by 1900, already begun a chaotic scramble for control of the infant industry. Who had a better claim to directing its affairs than he whose labor had done so much to create it in the first place? And with this, bear in mind that Thomas Edison was not always a narrowly-focused, professorial type. He was also a businessman of respectable talents, able to reason persuasively with colleagues in the boardroom. Although it is seldom mentioned in the standard biographies, he could be a gentleman of noble attributes and even charm, cordial, but firm and at his best before a knowledgeable audience whom he would fascinate with his unheard-of devices while inviting their ideas on how best to market them.

Edison combined scientific exactitude with commercial skills to fight hard for what his apologists regard as enlightened direction of this young, but promising movie industry which was by 1900 was sorely in need of a unifying leadership.

But any eulogistic description of Edison was howled down by a growing army of litigants nationwide seeking redress for what *they* saw as Edison's unseemly grasping for still-ripening fruits with a legal stranglehold meant to consign competition to outer darkness. Hardly the American way. Such contention eventuated in two armed camps, lawyers on either side waxing wealthy up the ladder to the higher courts, at every rung the litigants arguing their interpretations of Freedom and the right to uninhibited profit under the Constitution.

But very few, Edison included, could have predicted that the cheap nickelodeons of that day would mushroom into a phenomenon of

CHAPTER 1: EDISON'S INFLUENCE

dominating proportions such as motion pictures have ultimately become. Nor could anyone have guessed, with a welter of film studios sprouting up all over the East Coast, that the mecca of moviedom would be located anywhere but there.

2

From the East Coast to the West Coast

In the beginning, it was somewhere on the Eastern seaboard, where the population was heaviest and the great lending institutions were established, that logic directed the studios to be built. Philadelphia would have made sense, where the entrepreneur Sigmund Lubin had constructed a thoroughly modern affair, a first-class operation with a battalion of employees and opportunities for young executives and directors with vision.

But New York was the prime contender. Consider this: In 1890, there was not one amusement arcade in the city, whereas ten years later there were over a thousand, fifty of which were the new nickelodeons (the five-cent admission charge gave the novelty its name). By 1908, those fifty had become four hundred, occasionally with a barker and his megaphone out front collaring the passersby to come in and be amazed by something akin to a short filmstrip. At the outset, these had no story, no star, no plot, a mere toy by today's standards but so revolutionary that the impact proved bewildering to some, near hypnotic to a few, and sheer delight to virtually everyone. America had been smitten.

But even New York would be bypassed, for the center of gravity in the business world, as with the population, was edging inexorably westward. This was going forward in feverish haste as the last of the great opportunities for cheap acreage in America, still attracting settlers even from Europe, was fast drawing to a close. The new movie studios were caught up in this movement, and westward it had to be.

During the first decade of the twentieth century it was increasingly clear that the more ambitious studios would have to relocate somewhere on the West Coast. But to consider moving into embryonic Hollywood occurred to none of the film makers, for that village existed only as scattered orange groves. Nor was this the worst of its problems.

There is plenty of irony in the founding of that little settlement in 1887, for Hollywood had been intended by Horace and Daeida Wilcox not for the worship of money, but as a Methodist evangelistic center offering the Water of Life to a people given over to lingering visions of the Gold Rush era. Families with God-fearing, Bible-oriented pretensions found Hollywood and its controlled religious atmosphere a sweet savor. A number moved in and so augmented the conservative population that in 1903, the village could be incorporated as a city. There was rejoicing at the simultaneous adoption of laws strictly forbidding not only alcohol within city limits, but likewise theaters, nickelodeons, and all such enticements to Babylonian abandon. Not Edison nor anyone else would have taken their darling kinetoscopes into a place of such peril.

But with their attention fixated on the hereafter, Hollywood's city fathers failed to provide for the *here*. Their world turned upside down in 1910 when residents suffered a water shortage so severe that the administrators found it necessary to make the trip, hat in hand, to neighboring Los Angeles and beg the diversion of sufficient water to sustain their orange crops. Their request was granted, but the price of water was high; thenceforth the religious community was to exist as a satellite of the City of Angels. The move had cost Hollywood its independence. "Water of life" indeed!

Whether all this had been an answer to prayer or the devil's own handiwork depended on which side of the city line one resided. In any case, the statutes under which Hollywood had existed passed in review before the LA city council and were selectively rescinded to agree with the laws of the larger community. Hollywood's brief existence as a religious center thus ended abruptly, and the forces that recreated it as Tinsel-town were in the pulpit.

The Hollywood that we know today began evolving in the following year, 1911, with the advent of David Horsley, whom nobody remembers,

CHAPTER 2: FROM THE EAST COAST TO THE WEST COAST

and the city's first movie studio, of which nothing remains. Keystone barged in with its Komedy Kops in 1912, and Cecil B. DeMille with his crew found their way there to get away from Arizona and the sand that clogged their cameras. That was in 1913, by which time the Essanay Motion Picture enterprise was going great guns up in Fremont, far to the north, turning out dramas, comedies, and especially Westerns, and bringing each to a state of development on which Hollywood was later to capitalize.

But although Hollywood was transformed rapidly after 1913, at the turn of the century it was still true to the religious convictions of its founders. Let us go back to that time to pick up the thread of our story.

It was in those earliest years that the big cities of the Atlantic seaboard played host to studios mushrooming all over, those little beehives that would set up shop in storefronts and backlots. This author's father, Alden B. Parkhurst, was among those latter-day pioneers, having been the first to introduce motion pictures into the state of Maine. He and a friend, carting their gear in suitcases and slung over their shoulders, would horse-and-buggy it from Boston up into Maine's heartland and coastal regions for a back-slapping welcome by loggers and fishermen hungry for a little diversion. Long gone, all of them, but those tiny lights that failed did not fail to put their latest entertaining shows within reach of everybody in the country. By 1912, five million Americans could be found in nickelodeons daily and with the steady stream of technical improvements, plus the increasing polish of actors and directors, the sense of novelty was rapidly growing rather than wearing off.

THE ROAD ALMOST TAKEN

But virtually all of this frenetic activity was still in the East.

For an enterprise to actually locate west of the Mississippi and contend with a scanty labor pool and few local resources for cash or credit, it would have been visionary indeed, somewhere between foolhardy and ruinous.

However, then as always, California proved the grand exception to all rules, willing and able to set precedents suiting itself. The state's history from the outset has been an ongoing redefinition of the word "spectacular," routinely attracting the attention of the Western world for one thing after another. An American possession since 1848, thanks to Mexico's refusal to sell it to the Polk administration and the subsequent war that took it anyway, California welcomed the American newcomers by promptly yielding gold nuggets at Sutter's Mill to men who were not even looking for it. The electrifying news fairly flew to the other end of the country and then to the ends of the earth. The great, unstoppable Gold Rush then began, and within five fabulous years Californians were giving birth to their own version of the American Dream by unearthing almost 50% of the world's entire annual output of that mineral.

If we may expand the scope of our study just a bit, it is interesting to observe that the Spaniards had squatted on the land for centuries with no concept of the wealth underfoot, whereas a few enterprising Americans had uncovered the secret so swiftly that the world watched in wonderment and Madrid was stunned. Three centuries earlier, Spain had waxed sufficiently powerful with precious metals from the New World to dominate affairs on the European continent for over a hundred years. Mexican gold and Peruvian silver had equipped and paid the army that overran much of northern Europe, plus by 1588, a battle fleet before which England quailed, and the likes of which would not be seen again until the Allied cross-channel invasion of France in 1944. But now, ejected by combat boot from the American Southwest, Spain could only stammer in humiliation and witness the gold that might have been hers, and with which to launch yet another Spanish Century, enrich instead the treasury of a new breed of conquistadors. But there was no danger to the nations this time, inhibited both by temperament and by the Constitution from employing the newfound wealth for anything but internal development, to Americans the chimera of conquest and glory that was still popular in Europe was simply unthinkable.

To recount briefly, the 1849 gold rush so quickly filled our newly-acquired countryside with settlers of every stripe that California was emboldened to bypass the territorial stage of government altogether (never before, never again) and was accepted with full privileges of statehood by congressional acclamation in 1850. Such a tumultuous rush for a star on the flag, accomplished in a single year and with the most untidy such legislation ever, left a thousand loose administrative ends that occupied California's newly elected bureaucrats for the ensuing decade.

While the politicians were so occupied, ordinary Californians went about their lives doing what had to be done to civilize and modernize their portion of the West. The Union Pacific hurried its railroad to completion by 1869, employing battalions of immigrant Irish and Chinese who had come here for gold but had found only iron. With the railroad in operation, the population curve once more accelerated upward. San Francisco took on airs of self-importance both as the Western railroad terminal for the US and as a seaport looking toward the Far East– the tie that binds– opening commercial contact between New York and Yokohama and ending forever the necessity of frail wooden vessels threading the perilous Straits of Magellan.

In disorderly progression then, the be-whiskered frontiersman with his Kentucky rifle and later a Remington repeater, cleared a trail for the thin white line of Conestoga wagons loaded with families and their household basics. Into the settlements that soon dotted the trail came the lead officers to apportion homesteads to those who could afford a dollar or so per acre. Then came the courts of law which supplanted as quickly as was practicable the vigilante justice that had sometimes been necessary to restrain that lawless element by which frontier families all through history have been pestered.

Yet another frontier came next, this one of ranchers and farmers, and range wars ensued between the cattlemen whose livestock needed grass and the sheepherders whose flocks chewed the grass so close to the ground that there was nothing left for the steers. It was a situation crying out for mediation by sheriffs and the courts, but not relieved until 1875 with the invention of barbed wire.

By such rough justice the maturing West was readied for still another human wave, that of the enterprising businessmen who now might safely invest in building settlements into cities, workshops into industries, and dirt trails into the much-needed connecting highways. And always more railroads. When the Eastern business community could discern a survivable margin of profit, they likewise headed toward the sunset, predictably into California where the population was building and opportunity beckoned.

It was a thrilling and vibrant time to be alive in America if one could keep from being trampled, for what little remained of land for settlement after 1890 was fast disappearing to the trainloads of Easterners and immigrants. Still raw and thorny, the American West was no place for a weakling.

It was at this juncture, at what may be termed the onset of the "business frontier," that the camera crews set out on their own unique and colorful westward expansion.

3

Gilbert Anderson (AKA Bronco Billy)

The brief 1898 conflict that ushered Spain out of the international scene saw the United States under Theodore Roosevelt elbow its way to center stage. In the same year, Americans stampeded to the Klondike for yet another experience in gold, an auspicious beginning for the American Century.

Again in that year, the Edison Company with the great man himself in charge ventured into the first motion picture that can be called a Western. *Cripple Creek Bar Room* was a short one-reeler with no central character and no storyline, just tame goings-on before a stationary camera. A dozen or so men in Western attire came on-scene and with backs to the viewers poured themselves drinks and then strode off-camera. End of story. No Academy Awards here. Yet it was a beginning that was well received in the nickelodeons, and in which a few interested capitalists saw possibilities.

But possibility is not reality. It is wise to remind ourselves that those early efforts were merely a down payment on what that reality would eventually become. In our time we see the fulfillment of that century-old promise, and it is often marvelous to behold on the wide screen. But as we look at its modest beginnings, the temptation is to conclude that what was done back then was primitive, boring, and hardly worth the nickel that it cost to see it. True enough. These cracked and yellowed films are of only academic interest anymore. But even though it may require a wrench of the spirit to see value in them, remember that there was a time when those old pictures were likewise marvelous to behold.

Enter Broncho Billy.

There is no way to know if Gilbert M. Anderson, a Southerner residing in the east, was thinking Western at that time. Probably not. In '98 he was only fifteen. Born in Arkansas of Jewish parents in 1882, his real name was Max Aronson, which he altered to Gilbert M. Aronson when he and his sister began a stage career that flopped. The best position that the teenager could come up with was as a model for illustrators, capitalizing on a pretty good build. But that was no career for him. Before he was twenty, he changed his name yet again to Max Anderson, and finally to Gilbert M. Anderson to look better for a try in the new film industry.

But how would a name change improve his chances? Let's pause for a closer look at this.

Religious and ethnic overtones, then as now, gave a sick slant to much that was happening in the world and this country did not escape it. Unreasoned centuries old prejudice, entered our country with the shiploads of the mostly poor and steerage-class immigrants who came our way. Ellis Island was able to isolate communicable diseases but not bigotry,

CHAPTER 3: GILBERT ANDERSON (AKA BRONCO BILLY)

that most virulent and easily transmissible import from the old country.

Not that the immigrants found their new compatriots all that pure. Our own generation is largely unaware that the period of US history from the Civil War until the First World War was besmirched with racial and religious hatreds born and raised right here, issues that could draw blood and compared to today's ethnic problems turn pallid. A legacy from the days of slavery, lynching of blacks remained an accepted Southern institution, while the flood of new arrivals from Europe, especially from Ireland thanks to an 1846 famine of biblical proportions, made Roman Catholicism a target for intense animosity.

On the matter of Catholicism, Teddy Roosevelt in casual conversation once remarked that if he had his way, he would have taken Canada one way or another, thereby making us all one people. Look at Canada today, he went on, a social and industrial backwater making little contribution to world events; had their resources been added to ours, he argued, their country and ours would have been strengthened thereby.

He was then asked to look southward; would he, as president, also have taken Mexico, again, one way or another? Not a chance, was TR's response. And the reason? Because the Catholic religion of Mexico with its allegiance to Rome is totally incompatible with the entire history of our country. Trying to assimilate such a people, he argued, despite their many virtues, would throw an insupportable burden upon Americans while doing the Mexicans little or no good. In expressing such a viewpoint, Roosevelt perfectly reflected the temper of America at that time. That was then.

But then, as now, the uneducated and poor from Mexico, some still smarting over their government's failure to hold onto California, would cross the border hoping for a better life only to find that it came with a price tag too onerous to pay.

Thus, nearly all foreigners felt the heat in spite of the Statue of Liberty's sincere, yet sentimentalized, invitation to the world's huddled masses.

The trouble was that foreign families, despite their often excellent talents, washed up on our shores too many and too rapidly, an indigestible human mass with many resisting assimilation into the "melting pot". And with this, the Jewish people came in for their long-standing abuse. Some, like our hero, caved in to the point of disguising their names: anything to blend in, how else to make a living? There was, to be sure, a modicum of "melting" going on, but it was done grudgingly. And for those who tried to integrate, it was a practical matter, not religious and not ethnic.

It was this fellow Max Aronson who evolved into Broncho Billy Anderson, the first Golden Boy of motion pictures, pioneer of Western drama, and first of the international movie stars. Although he was not, himself, an immigrant, any number of Jewish people who came over on the black transports did find a welcome as they joined him for careers in film and the world of entertainment.

In 1902, fed up with wasting shoe leather as a traveling salesman, young Billy strode into the film studio of the Edison Company on 23rd St., New York, drawn thence by the magic of the inventor's name. Starry-eyed Anderson was hoping to start at the top and work up, and it was in that second-story studio that he got into this new field on the ground floor. A gentleman named Edwin S. Porter happened to be there that day. He was a balding, but still youngish director with Spielberg-like ambition and was soon to achieve lasting acclaim while other filmmakers just puttered along.

But until then, the modest scope of Porter's work with Edison had him merely cranking out single-reelers, and then shipping them off to make the rounds of the local nickelodeons. In this, he too was just puttering along. But that would soon change.

As the young man stood before his desk, the director eyed him as he would a slab of beef, turning him this way and that, making private judgments in the course of the interview. Porter toyed with the idea that Anderson might be just what he needed for a new venture of revolutionary dimensions then taking shape in his mind, provided the young man could cut it.

In those days, the studios did not insist upon impressive credentials or resumes; it was "what-you-see-is-what-you-get," and Anderson showed him a good specimen of a six-footer with obvious leadership qualities who could look the boss in the eye. Their discussion went well. Anderson was offered and readily accepted an acting part in an upcoming comedy, clearly intended by Porter as a screen test to prepare him for that darling brainstorm of his, a picture that would hasten the evolution of motion pictures as nothing had previously done.

And his qualifications for an acting career? With zero Broadway experience, slender indeed. His face was not that of a great matinee attraction but it was capable of a convincing scowl or a boyish grin, which he could exaggerate to convey the message of a script in the era before sound. And he had about him a disarming aura that later proved an asset in holding together the variegated characters he picked up along the road to serve as extras in his Westerns and comedies.

So Porter gave Anderson a nice part in *The Messenger Boy's Mistake*, horseplay over a young man's embarrassment when pajamas instead of flowers are delivered to his girlfriend, very risqué by prevailing Victorian standards. The newcomer, oozing potential, did well and was invited to remain.

Having perhaps found his man, Porter felt encouraged to go ahead with his plans for a real thriller. And by coincidence, in the same year of 1902, a headline-grabbing event took place that further prepared the public for the venture upon which Porter would cash in. Butch Cassidy and the Sundance Kid became notorious in newspapers around the country. Bank robbers Robert LeRoy Parker and Henry Langbaugh, their real names, in the company of a young schoolteacher, Etta Place, fled from the West to New York with $30,000 in stolen money, then to South America and death in a blaze of gunfire. These were "the last of the badmen," bank and train robbers in the tradition of Jesse and Frank James, and they certainly caught the public's imagination.

But they were anachronisms from a generation or so earlier when proper law enforcement had yet to catch up with the fast-moving frontier. By 1902, the West had settled down to something other than shoot-outs and range law. Nonetheless, people persisted in their romantic involvement with that departed era, avidly following the newspaper accounts of the two gunslingers. They became almost lovable. On today's wide screen, Robert Redford and Paul Newman with tolerable adherence to the historical outline (not always prized by film-makers), recreated Cassidy and the Kid in a manner to assure their continued endearment.

And so it was back then. The two train robbers caught and held the attention of the public, and none of this was lost upon Edwin S. Porter. Theatergoers responded like sheep being led by newspaper headlines toward his new production, *The Great Train Robbery*, another Edison-Porter production, and this time with an entertaining, even shocking story. It was a serious attempt at realism. Eight hundred feet of film and the unheard-of length of thirteen minutes made it the longest reel to come from any studio. It was also the industry's first movie with a plot.

Anderson lied to Porter that he could ride a horse, was allowed to join the outlaws as they barreled down the railroad track, was then seen wild-eyed with terror before being thrown, and looked pretty sheepish as he faced the boss, steaming among the cameras. That he was not fired tells us something about Porter. But now that he had overreached himself, Anderson hastened to get some real he-man practice by mounting a saddle attached to a wooden sawhorse in the New Jersey studio. He eventually got the hang of it, but not by that method. This unintended comedy proved one of those eggs from which mighty things have hatched, the event that initiated the cycle of the Western movies.

The truth about his riding ability was quickly discovered, but even so Porter allowed Anderson another part. He at least was game enough to attempt something at which he might break his neck. As it turned out, Anderson had several small parts in that film (there were no big ones), that of a bandit, a fireman, and as a passenger on the train. He began his list of movie "firsts," being the first man shot to death in front of a camera, high drama indeed and with genuine impact upon viewers innocent of previous experience with bloodshed. As the passengers were herded together outside the coach, Anderson made a dash for freedom. Receiving a blank in the back, he writhed, staggered, and fell face down as Edison's stock went up.

This old film is today regarded as the first "masterpiece," if we may stretch the term, in a long line of such that still continues. Every discovery on this untraveled course, and *The Great Train Robbery* made several of them, was the kind of early growth that had to be experienced for the art form to develop. Rarely does recognition crown the first efforts of a pioneer on an untried path. With this picture, his first and only production of importance, Porter achieved a significant goal, but pioneered no more.

The Great Train Robbery had a remarkable affect upon Anderson. From that time on he was committed to motion pictures to the exclusion of all else. He then set about learning every aspect of the work from acting to editing to managing, from tearing down a camera to putting it together. And thanks to his part in the picture, he had caught the attention of other studios whose execs frequented the nickelodeons to see what their enemies were doing.

A position came his way from the Vitagraph Company in Manhattan so Anderson left, with Edison's and Porter's blessing, to assume it. This was a young man in a hurry. Hired by Vitagraph as a director, with the informal organization of the time, he was free to broaden his experience as an actor, script writer, cameraman and executive, at a salary of twenty-five dollars a week. Now, that was real money.

In 1904, *Raffles, The Amateur Cracksman*, the story of a thief, added to his successes, and two years later he resigned from Vitagraph when theater owners John Harris and Henry Davis hired him to make one- and two-reelers, and that put him into production; he was still a freshman, but learning. It was the usual thing for owners of theater chains to make their own movies and show them on their own circuits.

But his stay there was brief, and 1907 found him in Chicago, which was as far west as the industry had thus far gone. Unattached and footloose, this was a good upward move for him. There he worked with several outfits in succession, including that of Colonel Selig, a wealthy producer whose title was as theatrical as his one-reelers.

But with all this, the public acceptance of *The Great Train Robbery* never left his mind. It was the best motion picture yet, and its continuing popularity insisted that the public was anxious for more.

He was reminded of this waiting opportunity again when he made a business trip for Selig into Colorado. While relaxing on the train and gazing idly through the windows, Billy was impressed by the kaleidoscope of deserts, clouds and horizons, and even more impressed that it had not occurred to a single studio to exploit it. The big city studios were content to produce Eastern Westerns, simulating scenery with mountains and cactus sketched on plywood or even on cardboard. The simplest peasant could see that the backgrounds were phony, but audiences never complained about it, so cardboard it remained.

But with the genre of pictures then edging into Billy's mind, those cheap, unconvincing sets stood squarely in the way of realism. With the glorious American West free for the taking, it was high time for the film industry to get out of the big cities. Increasingly, Anderson was getting his mind, although not yet his hands, on the controls.

4
S&A Becomes Essanay

The future Broncho Billy was working up an appetite for distance. If he could separate himself from the Eastern offices, two things would be accomplished. He would have a free rein and authority over his own operation, and the incomparable scenery would lend a cutting edge to his pictures that competing studios could never match. And incredibly, not one studio had dared–a classic study of inertia–to send their camera crews into the mountains or the deserts. But this had to be just around the corner; one producer or another would eventually come around to the idea. Anderson was anxious to be the first.

But it was in the East where the film industry was doing well, that the money was entrenched. And before the money would move, the ex-salesman would have to market his plan. Chicago was as far west as the industry had ventured. Although hardly prototypes of either Fremont or the future Hollywood, at least three companies in Chicago continued turning a profit on the standard ten-minute one-reelers: William Selig, George Kleine and George Spoor.

The first person to whom Anderson broached his idea was Selig, being already in his employ. The Colonel listened but was underwhelmed. He proved apathetic, even quarrelsome, and young Anderson did not have sufficient ballast to convince him. Billy's persistence was getting him nowhere, with Selig jumping up and down in refusal to detach a part of his crew to break new ground at a distance from his personal control. So, he gave up on the old goat.

Billy's experience in managerial savvy was incomplete. He had not yet made himself indispensable. As for Selig, he was a good businessman, but he had no vision. And this meant, of course, that he was not a good businessman.

There are two kinds of luck and now the good one came his way. Billy was still a-bubble with his new-found love for western scenery when he made acquaintance with one George K. Spoor, a distributor of motion picture equipment who had wherewithal in abundance along with an indispensable open mind. In the course of conversations in Spoor's office or over a buffalo steak dinner, the smell of success for each of them grew stronger. Anderson found Spoor surprisingly easy to convince, for unbeknownst to this young enthusiast, Billy was a visionary who would fit very nicely into Spoor's business plans for the near future.

Together they cut a deal. As they worked it out, Spoor would provide the financial backing and manage the home studio in Chicago while Anderson, all smiles, agreed to direct a roving Western branch with the option of settling into any location that suited him. The bargain was struck, the papers were signed, and the conference ended in good-natured camaraderie.

Although this arrangement is given little or no emphasis in the standard histories, Billy had crossed a rubicon that proved significant, not only for his personal career, but for the evolution of the industry. In what had become an arena of gladiators, he and Spoor clinked glasses over their spanking-new and strongly muscled contender. Together they created the new Essanay Film Manufacturing Company, the name being a play on their initials, featuring Spoor in the leading role with the key to the cash register and Anderson in support. Wall Street took notice that energy and drive had united with powerful financial backing to advance the S&A logo immediately into the front rank of the movers and shakers.

That was in 1907, and was preparatory to what was coming next.

CHAPTER 4: S&A BECOMES ESSANAY

5

Impact of the of Sherman Antitrust Act

In strict secrecy with Edison and other important film studios, Spoor had agreed to attend a planned backroom arrangement with international implications that would surely destabilize the motion picture industry nationwide. On paper, Thomas Edison's plan balanced a measure of risk against a near certainty of great wealth. The inventor's towering reputation made it possible for him to propose such a venture.

But such a move might also bring the machinery of government down upon the necks of everyone involved. This was understood, but Edison, in consultation with his attorneys, pronounced the risks acceptable. The pioneering had already been done and great industries had been reared by such as Rockefeller, Carnegie, Morgan and a host of others. They had taken the same risk with success and with profit.

Edison was aiming at a monopoly of his own, of the motion picture industry with himself as chairman of the board. A total of ten movie producers, heretofore in competition, were invited to act in cooperation under his leadership. The hook, if it may be called that, was generously baited, and the movie magnates were prepared to listen.

Thanks to the Civil War, great strength had accrued in the government in Washington. And thanks to the same cause, great strength had also been garnered by the business community. Between them, they had shared the responsibility for arming, equipping, transporting and leading the armies that brought victory. This created an unspoken alliance between the federal government and big business, to the exclusion of the common people, that promised and delivered victory during the war, but also promised and delivered nothing but trouble for the years of peace that followed. In effect, one war was followed almost immediately by another of a different kind, a nearly epic class struggle between Big Business, with the connivance of Congress and the courts, against labor unions and emerging smaller enterprises.

A significant part of the movie industry was coaxed into this through the projected facts and figures presented by Edison and his attorneys. It mattered little that they might be on a collision course with the White House.

. . . . .

During the Gilded Era of the 1870s and '80s, government agencies had to give attention to the increasing appeals by small businesses looking to Washington for much-needed relief. By 1890, Congress finally threw a sop to the voters with the passage of the Sherman Antitrust Act. Ostensibly this gave the presidency legislation needed to act on behalf of the citizenry by reining in the trusts.

But a glance at the lopsided congressional vote is revealing. The Senate voted 51 to 1 in favor of the bill. The House of Representatives weighed in at 242 to zero, a most unbalanced and overwhelming tally. It was first hailed by the man in the street as a victory for the people, but reading between the lines, the picture becomes both clear and alarming. The entire Congress, with the exception of one senator, passed a severe piece of legislation against Big Business. But would the Senate and the House, by and large at the service of the moneyed class, pass a law contrary to their own best interests?

Not likely. Considering that Congress in point of fact represented the great trusts and monopolies more than it did the country at large and that the legislators themselves were not only among the stockholders, but many of them owed their very positions in the nation's capital to unfailing support from the business world. At least one successful businessman, Mark Hanna of Ohio, entered politics specifically to see to it that the great monopolies did not lose their grip on Congress. The Republican and Democratic parties therefore did nothing to remove the causes of popular discontent.

CHAPTER 5: IMPACT OF THE OF SHERMAN ANTITRUST ACT

When it dawned upon the working class that they had no representation in the nation's capital, they recalled the lessons from their school textbooks that this was a primary cause of the American Revolution, and the prospect before them was bleak. Regarding the Sherman Antitrust Act as among the most insincere, one might say deceptive, bills ever written into law, in some cities they took to the streets.

To underscore this, the McKinley administration refused to invoke the law at all. The antitrust act became useless, destined for an unpredictable future.

Working people had been looking to it for impressive victories against the railroads, iron and steel, the magnates of the coal mines and against that ogre of finance J.P. Morgan, envisioning each of them hooked and dragged out of the arena trailing blood while some of their money trickled back to the small businesses. But this did not come to pass until 1902, after McKinley had been removed from office by an assassin's bullet and Roosevelt had put his hand to the helm.

Whether or not the law would be enforced for the benefit of the people would depend upon the nature of the man in the White House.

It is beyond the parameters of our study to describe further that tennis ball called the Sherman Act except to say that during TR's tenure of office, there were indeed some notable victories for the people as great financial and industrial concerns were broken up and dragged piecemeal out of the arena.

But after 1909, with the Trust Buster's sword then hung on the wall and Howard Taft deemed a complaisant successor, Big Business might once more aspire to remain standing after the usual legal swordplay. Corporate management was looking toward a reaffirmation of its own specialized definition of freedom under the Constitution.

It was during this alarming period that Edison invited Essanay with several other strong firms, and in strict secrecy, to unite their fortunes into a trust, guarding their interests against all other studios, which the newspapers referred to as the "Independents." Spoor's millions qualified him for a chair in the boardroom, and 1908 saw the creation of the Motion Picture Patents Company.

The very definition of legalized financial power, the trust was composed of ten companies, initiates into the inner mysteries. Edison was its guiding spirt, along with Vitagraph, Biograph, Essanay, Kalem, Lubin, and Selig, with two French firms, Pathe and Meleis, plus George Klein as distributor, an impressive polygon of power. The trust-busters in Washington marked it for eventual attention and kept a wary eye on it, but the Patents Company had anticipated that.

From the outset, the trust was girded about by a corps of the finest New York and Chicago attorneys that money could buy, and with this the unholy ten expected to relax behind the battlements while the profits rolled in.

It can be troubling to a historian that a national icon such as Thomas Alva Edison would subscribe to a course of action that our generation would regard as unethical. And yet, at every step the new law was scrupulously complied with; it was all perfectly legal. And a case can be made that there was no evil intent, that in this as in all previous encounters between the federal government and the large corporations, the nation itself was simply working out the direction it wanted to take. That direction would not be clear until a great deal of litigation had run its course.

Lauren Bacall, looking back upon her own acting career in a February 1999 interview, pronounced upon the entire history of the industry when she said, "What I don't like about it is the general mentality.…It's only about money." Judged by this standard, Edison for all his ethics, was tarnished.

In any case, the inventor agreed to supply the machines to his coterie and for this was paid a royalty. All patents were pooled in a cozy arrangement that intended no mercy for the Independents.

And then the Eastman Company was induced to join, agreeing to sell film to the brethren and to no others, making the Patents Company a universe unto itself. Intrigue, or shall we say confidentiality, had played an unseemly role.

Announced to the surprised business world on January 1, 1909, the obvious power of this monster evoked a monument howl of "an evil," "unfair practices" and "un-American" from the unorganized competition which thereupon organized to set legal machinery in motion to dismember it. Was the trust illegal? That would remain undetermined until, as everybody expected, the Supreme Court would render its decision. But it took years for the case to seep upward to that level, and in the meanwhile the Patent Company's stock maintained its ascent.

More importantly, the uninhibited artistic promise of motion pictures, at least within the cartel, now shot forward. As with any endeavor, organization and unity of purpose are everything and the Patents Company had both. For the next several years the members of the trust while enjoying high profits were also the heavy lifters of the industry. To those on the inside it was a fine illustration of the American Way as guaranteed by the Constitution.

That was one point of view.

The other viewpoint had it that right in the middle of the trust-busting spree initiated by Roosevelt, eleven companies domestic and foreign had the temerity to defy the law of the land, thenceforth to march in lockstep and trample competition. This was the American Way gone haywire and exactly what Roosevelt had hoped to forestall by enforcing legislation enacted during his own and previous terms. Hosts of one-horse studios now faced oblivion due to being denied access to film, cameras, and actors and much else.

As for which of these interpretations was better for the country, the reader may make his own choice.

Those pompous magnates of the early movie industry, be it said on their behalf, at least gave to the country something of tangible value. Is there anyone whose life has not been touched by the influence, even the grandeur, of motion pictures? Surely not. In the same way, consider the continental railroads, the iron and steel industry, America's great financial houses and more, blessings that positioned our country head and shoulders above the rest of the world and delivered unto us the twentieth century. This inheritance came to our generation without effort on our part, bequeathed to us by men, sinners all, perhaps disgraced by malfeasance of one kind or another, men who, by today's standards, would be hauled before the bar of justice to face prison. And yet, their material contributions were on a magnificent scale, surely to redeem them when contrasted with today's stock market paper-shufflers into double-book-keeping artistry, men on the take who would gladly leave us with nothing.

6

Broncho Billy Prevails

It was about this time that Anderson's public persona was invented. As he told it forthrightly in 1958, "I happened to read a story by Peter Kyne with a character called 'Broncho Billy,' and I stole the name for the films. Later I met Kyne and he said it was all right. We never bought anything in those days."

Then he made efforts to find an actor who could play this new role with conviction, trying out one amateur after another. It should have been a snap because voice quality was never a factor and there was no script to be memorized. Anderson, the sort of director who encouraged people to work with him rather than for him, urged each volunteer to "just be yourself" before the camera, but stage fright was on everybody's back. Nobody could get it right so he had a go at it himself, as if he didn't have enough to do already. He got himself into cowboy gear and acted out a short story he had hurriedly written. That film, like so many of his other creations, is now lost and nobody has a clue about what the story was.

He shipped it back to his partner in Chicago and waited for Spoor's nod of approval before doing anything more with it. Spoor sent back word that the film was being well received in the local theaters, and that report turned Anderson loose for the next several years to grind out Westerns like link-sausages.

The first Broncho Billy picture, a one-reeler, was forthcoming that same year, 1908, and it set the moral tone for every last Western of his that followed. Entitled, *The Bandit Makes Good*, it was a conversion story of a criminal who changed his ways. There were several hundred of these happy-ending pictures before the series ended in 1915 and a few of the titles reveal a pattern that rendered all of those films perfectly acceptable to theatergoers and especially to parents:

Broncho Billy's Sermon
Broncho Billy's Christmas Deed
Broncho Billy's Gratefulness
When Love and Honor Called
Broncho Billy's Teachings
Broncho Billy's Bible
The Badman's Downfall
Broncho Billy's Word of Honor
Broncho Billy's Redemption

This was a remarkably narrow dramatic range, but gauged by the gate receipts, the public never tired of it and in the trade magazines a negative review of the Broncho Billies was more or less unheard of.

On the other hand, there was no such narrowness to be found in Essanay's filming methods and script material, and upon this Billy latter commented upon Western movies generally, "They're just like I used to make, except that they talk a little. Most of them are mediocre. The all have the same formula, two guns, bullets, 'pardner,'…. horses and a sheriff. It's one big stew out of the same stew pot." In 1992, historian William Everson seconded the motion with the verdict that Billy "…. had pioneered everything that was taking place before the cameras."

7
Westward Migration

Anderson's roving company consisted at first only of himself, one cameraman and the comedian Ben Turpin, an actor whose personal warmth was to make him a truly beloved character in early movie history.

From 1908 to 1912 this tiny unit migrated from one place to another, trying to decide upon a permanent home, preferably near a railroad to keep communication open to Chicago. In the days before artificial lighting, daylight was critical and locations were chosen according to the number of "shooting days" they could expect, and this limited Anderson and company to the Southwest.

The trio gathered speed picking up cowboys along the way, and by 1912 numbered over fifty. Unlike Billie, these were the real thing, lean, hard-riding cowpokes, experts in the saddle, but glad to put distance between themselves and a man-killing profession on the range for the sheer fun and better pay of the films. There were no stunt men on the Essanay lot, and the cowboys performed their sometimes dangerous riding over broken ground at the risk of being bloodied while about it. Several of Anderson's riders were among the finest horsemen then living.

Anderson kept them all busy during daylight hours acting out stories he would put together the night before. They pushed on from Chicago to Colorado and then to California. The summer of 1911 was given to shooting scenes at San Rafael and shipping the completed reels back to the home office. Before they packed up to leave, the chamber of commerce spread a farewell banquet for actors and technicians with an invitation to make a permanent home there. An old newswriting expression comes to mind: "A good time was had by all."

Billy fell into the pattern of writing out the essentials of a story at night when things were quiet, everything flowing from his imagination. He would brief his actors the next morning, filming the scenes without further ado and only the sketchiest rehearsal or no rehearsal at all. There was rarely a problem with this in the days before sound.

Those who have taken the trouble to study Anderson's contribution have been amazed at his prolific output. No other studio could equal it. Hundreds of completed scripts came forth in as many weeks, and in periods of what must have been feverish activity, a picture a day.

It surely seems that such quantity must have had an unfortunate impact upon quality, and one frankly wonders if the pictures were worth watching. For a contemporary opinion we turn to a trade journal, *The Moving Picture World,* May 15, 1909, in which the writer voted two thumbs and a big toe up in reviewing a new Essanay release, quoted here without deletion:

> A MEXICAN'S GRATITUDE...*An Essanay film which had some thrilling scenes and is certain to please the average audience wherever it is shown. There is life and action without bloodshed and the melodramatic features are made attractive rather than repulsive. The story is that a Mexican is saved from being hanged as a horsethief by the sheriff. He writes the word "Gratitude" on a card, tears it in two, gives one half to the sheriff and keeps the other half himself. Years afterward this same sheriff falls in love with a girl of the West. She is also wanted by a cowboy and he contrives to bring the sheriff and another girl together, and gets the girl the sheriff loves there just in time to see him in the scheming girl's embrace. Explanations are impossible, and he sees the girl he wants walk away with the false cowboy. The sheriff has a fight with him and forces him to confess his treachery. The cowboy goes to a Mexican's hut and secures the services of two greasers to do his bidding. The three lie in wait for the sheriff and his sweetheart, overpower them and drag them away to the Mexican's hut where the cowboy exults for a time and then forces the girl into another room.*

CHAPTER 7: WESTWARD MIGRATION

The Mexican wants some tobacco and sees a sack projecting from the sheriff's pocket. In pulling it out, he pulls out the half of the card with the word "Gratitude" upon it. When the cowboy returns to the room he is comparing the card. He then asks the sheriff if that was given him by a man whom he saved from lynching a few years before. The sheriff replies that it was. Whereupon the Mexican immediately loosens the sheriff's bonds, and a fight between the sheriff and the cowboy ensues. The sheriff has him across the table choking him into insensibility when the girl appears and begs him to stop, and the two go away together.

It is impossible to invest this story in telling with the life that is in the picture. It seems as though the characters were going to speak, they do their parts so naturally, while the staging is remarkably good. The film was heartily applauded in two theatres where it was seen the past week, and everyone who attends motion picture shows know that applause is somewhat rare.

The word "racist" was not in the country's vocabulary when that was written. By today's sensitive standard, the language here would be regarded as intemperate, but it passed without comment back then. The derogatory term "greaser" (with the 's' pronounced as a 'z') went into obsolescence sometime before World War II. How times change, occasionally for the better.

A modern critic adds to the above his own thoughtful appraisal: "Billy made intense, if simplistic, little moral dramas…filled with action and a straight-forward, unabashed heroism. The best of them may yet claim the modern viewer's attention." Those early films, expressing as they did an almost biblical idealism were extremely popular, in part because that idealism resonated then as it seldom does with audiences now.

Gate receipts at five and ten cents each did wonders for the stock market. In 1911, the General Film Company, which included the Spoor-Anderson enterprise, released figures of total net profits after payment of dividends to the individual studios. The breakdown for the Motion Picture Patents Company caused cork-popping and back-slapping all around.

Pathe-Freres . . $165,000
Vitagraph 150,000
Edison. 123,000
Selig 110,000
Biograph 105,000
Essanay 102,000
Lubin 101,000
Kalem 91,000
Kleine 77,000
Meleis 31,000

George Spoor back in the home office had every reason to glow, for this was big money. However, as will be seen later, financial success was having a perverse effect upon the senior partner that Anderson could not have foreseen. Instead of encouraging a venturesome spirit, Spoor was gradually slipping into a siege mentality. Let's hold the line; let's not take risks with innovations; let's not upset this lovely apple-cart. Eventually his attitude set like cement, but it was not a problem for Anderson just yet.

Broncho Billy's impact upon the movies in general and upon the Western in particular has been termed "immeasurable," and rightly so. At the risk of overpraise, let's explore further one aspect of his work usually missed by critics, hence passed by without comment.

It is that in every Broncho Billy picture justice and fair play triumphed. Likewise were the softer virtues of warmth, decency and humanity. In many of the Hollywood and TV productions of our time, with increasing emphasis upon what can only be called lurid X-ratings and the ascendancy of forces that could well mark America as a post-Christian nation, historians have observed that none of this could be found in the Essanay productions, nor in the work of the next generation of Western stars, many of whom drew inspiration from the pacesetting Broncho Billy films. The elevated tone of his one- and two-reelers is reflected in the work of William S. Hart, Tom Mix, Harry Carey, Hoot Gibson, Tim McCoy, Buck Jones, and from these down to Audie Murphy and John Wayne. Some of the later actors polished a particular virtue to a high gloss. Thus,

CHAPTER 7: WESTWARD MIGRATION

Roy Rogers would never kiss the heroine before the camera (although he did reserve the right to kiss his horse), and no silver bullet of the Lone Ranger's guns ever killed a man; spilling no blood, he would only shoot the weapon from an outlaw's hand. All of which was premeditated guidance for young viewers.

But these examples are variations on the theme first played by Broncho Billy. His pictures were uniformly wholesome, and parents were not fearful of what their children would have thrust upon them at the nickelodeon or the early theaters.

Artistically speaking, it would not have been easy to improve upon the Broncho Billies considering the limitations under which all studios in those days had to operate. Even if one makes the strained comparison between Anderson and Hart– strained because Hart had Anderson's films to analyze and improve upon– it is remarkable that Hart did not carry the Western beyond the level of accomplishment set by Billy. In this writer's judgment, Anderson's pictures were superior both in storyline and in overall credibility.

The great bulk of those films has been lost. "Kids burned them up," says Fremont resident Art Fereira today, as they rampaged years later through the hollow shell of the old studio. They located the vault beneath the floor and thoughtlessly destroyed a precious link between the past and the present. Nitrate decomposition wiped out much of the remainder. The largest extant collection, oddly enough, is in England, with very few films on this side of the Atlantic. Some may yet be found in libraries or in guarded private collections, or may rest undiscovered in dusty attics and basements. Those that remain to us are among the most fascinating relics of the early twentieth century.

* * * * *

Billy put his people to good use, sending men with camera experience to seek out the best locations for future filming. One of this scouts, Jess Robbins, brought word of an ideal spot then known as Niles, not far from Oakland and San Francisco, potential reservoirs for actors. Everything was within easy riding distance including a perfect canyon with a babbling brook, rocky chasms, wooded slopes and a jagged, photogenic skyline.

This writer for years has been up and down those hills and knows them well. Robbins also had praise for the rustic dirt roads, the railroad, the rolling hills, and the nearby ocean, a neat package of every necessary item that Anderson just had to investigate.

It was then that a high-tech and dynamic industry moved in, bag and baggage, on one of the sleepiest villages in the West.

8
Long Term Relationship with Niles Begins

The essence of obscurity in those days was the tiny agricultural village of Niles (resisting extinction today as a mere district of Fremont). The town and the now-forgotten Essanay Movie Studio (extinct altogether) never "married" but began a "long-term relationship" to inscribe in celluloid an account of what can happen when an irresistible force meets an immovable object. The LTR began in 1912, the year the Titanic disaster grabbed the headlines and just prior to that evil era in which unimaginable violence scorched the page of history, a final moment of collective innocence before the torrent of blood that we know as the First World War.

But our concern here is with more congenial matters, like the torrent of one-reelers released to a waiting public and the flood of cash that was generated when this ambitious studio descended upon a conservative township that had not, financially nor in any other way, budged an inch in many years.

But the "force" was not really irresistible, nor was the "object" all that immovable, for the two tried and succeeded at a most interesting accommodation.

These four tumultuous years would resurrect a clutch of colorful personalities, budding actors and actresses with high-flying pretensions, cigar-chomping execs often with more money than brains who fancied themselves in charge, and energetic young directors who fancied themselves free to manage as they pleased. All of which served to create a lot of fuss and feathers and, for the town of Niles, a sufficient cash-flow to support the whole population and to encourage near-complete dependence of the community upon the studio.

And in that fleeting span of four years the impact of this particular studio upon motion pictures *per se* has proved enduring even to our own time.

"Essanay Firm With Fifty-Two Employees Choose This Spot as Most Suitable for Pictures," crowed the *Township-Register* on April 6, 1912:

> *Niles, April 6. With a payroll of several hundred dollars a week and a company of fifty-two artists and helpers, the Essanay Film Company of Chicago located in Niles this week and will stay at least three months, coming here to make moving picture films of which this company is one of the best-known manufacturers in the world.*

The husky six-footer in a salt-and-pepper suit stepped off the train and looked around, squinting into the sun, followed by a miscellany of humanity with piles of suitcases, trunks and boxes.

The pretty country maid regarded the newcomer in wonderment.

The city fellow pulled down his straw hat to shield his eyes, a perfect day for filming, and asked a country boy for the nearest hotel. It was but a short walk away, right across the unpaved street.

With no immediate need for money, Anderson's first act seems odd. Within a day or so of arrival, he took up a collection among the townsfolk to rent an empty barn on Mortimer's lot as a temporary studio. Who knows? He may have been testing the temper of the town toward his new enterprise. He kept a record of the contributors and urged his people to patronize their businesses. With Mortimer's barn for indoor work, stalls for their sixteen horses plus a railway car on a siding for processing film, the company was soon humming. Big Business had begun its takeover.

Then as now, the making of a movie was a colorful phenomenon in which the work seemed more like play, as in a sense it was, and with more gold at the end of its rainbow than one could glean in a lifetime of clerking or shoeing horses. That so much profit could be so much fun seemed almost immoral, and that was no small part of the magic.

Some of the townspeople muttered that the movies would bring

CHAPTER 8: LONG TERM RELATIONSHIP WITH NILES BEGINS

in slick-talking "outsiders" and high-toned women and that the whole shebang could corrupt the young. But all America was under the spell of this new plaything, and to a degree not to be seen again until the advent of the computer.

Few people took it seriously as an art form, as an industry, or as anything more profound than entertainment at that early stage, but it had certainly grabbed the nation by the eyes. The great cities of the East had succumbed; was it any wonder that this little village was swept away? Besides, as Anderson pointed out to the city fathers, wherever this industry made its home, financial profit would ooze like honey to the edges of the town.

Continuing social ferment witnessed changes in the rural/urban balance of the country, changes so profound that the topsy-turvy existence of Niles, which is to say early Fremont, after 1912 proved a microcosm reflecting what had been happening in America as a whole. Since the Civil War, various factors had been conspiring to ensure that the city population would grow at an explosive rate at the expense of the farming districts and the thinly-populated countryside. For one thing, European immigration never abated and most looked for big-city jobs on the Eastern seaboard. For another, the urban birthrate had been far surpassing that of the farming communities, ensuring an eventually heavier voter turnout. And again, the enticements to a better income in the cities was drawing the young people away from the old homesteads and into the factories.

All of which made the handwriting on the wall plain even to the uneducated: No longer would delegates from rural America, diminishing in number at each election, exercise their customary dominance of the halls of Congress. America was being overtaken by the growing preponderance of voters in the cities.

The population shift was elbowing the farming communities into political eclipse. But as its dying star flickered, its brilliance never to return, the political hopes of rural America right at this time exploded into a supernova by the silver-tongued oratory of William Jennings Bryan. On three occasions, in 1896, 1900 and 1908, the Great Commoner, the final and most eloquent voice for rural America, lost presidential elections to candidates who drew their political strength from the ever-burgeoning cities. Analysts at the time and since could only shake their heads in dismay, concluding that Bryan might have made a splendid president, but that he represented a cause already lost. On the other hand, that which had barged in on Fremont in the form of a motion picture studio was the wave of the future.

9

Industrial Age Hardships

For the first decade or so, despite their popularity, by no means were the movies universally approved. And there were mixed feelings on this even among the actors, for while the more spirited ones were ambitious for public recognition, others preferred to simply blend into the background. Een though the films were prominently attractive many actors felt insensitive with their identities becoming known as they believed doing scenes before a camera was a step backwards from the regular stage productions.

All of which has less to do with the theater than it does with human nature. Radio broadcasting, a newcomer in the 1920s just as films had been a decade earlier, also suffered and for the same reason. Stanford Mirkin, author of *What Happened When*, remarks that "…stars of theater and music did not consider radio a suitable medium for first-class talent." It appears that any flouting of tradition inspires some of us to raise our eyebrows in supercilious dismissal.

But the extraordinary expansion of the picture industry is not to be wondered at, considering that overnight maturation had become routine for the whole of American industry. There was a legion of powerful business concerns already in place by the time the Patents Company joined the lineup as a latecomer. Edison's monopoly did not break new ground, as that had already been done by the great industrial combinations that arose during the explosive development in the business world after the Civil War. As far back as 1853, one Erastus Corning organized a scattering of fourteen short railroad lines to create the New York Central, possibly the first corporate merger in US history. Others soon followed, with combinations seemingly destined to be in competition and sometimes at war with each other, with embryonic labor unions, even with the American people when profits were at stake.1 Increasingly, this became obvious with Congress and the White House when Washington finally, by 1890, made a gesture toward the relief of the people with the aforementioned Sherman Antitrust Act.

A hostile, bristling landscape it could be when viewed by the man in the street who could buy coal in winter only at inflated prices, by tiny household industries competing with company outlets under impossible pricing conditions, by the mom-and-pop enterprises struggling to put a son through college, by movie studios with one camera and two employees denied the right to buy film at any price. People today, in the 21st century, know nothing of the heartaches so commonplace back then, for the energy it took for America to adjust to the Industrial Age was expended by our great-grandfathers who had to live with it. And the mighty monopolies, with no restraints except those that were self-imposed, thought it necessary to ignore the complaints of the citizenry for they were engaged in a larger war against each other. They could afford no tears for the common people. This is what is meant by the adjective that had found its way into editorials and everyday speech – "ruthless."

But although they similarly had no love for each other, the great companies reserved their most virulent hatred for any threatened curtailment of their ideas of democracy, which is to say financial profit. And so, we have the power of the iron and steel trust, of Standard Oil, of the American Sugar Refining Company, the insurance trust, the concrete combine, the National Biscuit Company, the great leather monopoly, and a host of aspiring lesser combinations, all of which formed a magnificent capitalistic backdrop for this new entry, Thomas Edison's Motion Pictures Patents Company.

And tucked away amid all this firepower, if we look closely, we may see Spoor and Anderson and the Essanay Motion Picture Studios.

While they remained untaxed and unbridled during the whole of the Gilded Era, the imperious captains of industry presumed to be laws unto themselves, and with hardly any exaggeration, nation-states within the nation. Whatever was best for the company was best for the country they expected the national government to be at their service and with that, they had grown too big for their britches. Their legitimacy had little to do with the Constitution. It was purely Darwinian with frontier feral instincts clothed anew for boardroom respectability but atavistic nonetheless, a throwback to a time which the country thought it had outgrown.

"To the rising capitalist," observes the historian Harold Faulkner in discussing the period following the Civil War, "and in fact to the average citizen, it seemed not only unnecessary but bad economics to regulate private capital. Capital should be aided, not impeded, in the development of the vast natural resources of which, it was believed, there was a sufficiency for all…" But Faulkner adds that there was a growing uneasiness across the country over "the control of the federal government by the business interests during most of the period after 1860."

The corporations when at their worst felt justified in defying the country at large and in ignoring the informal pleas of the federal government during the White House's early, tentative efforts toward accommodation. In 1910, the nation was compared by the sharp-eyed William Archer to "an enormously rich country overrun by a horde of robber barons, and very inadequately policed by the central government…" But all of this was new ground, and the government was unsure of its right or its responsibility to interfere in private business.

But there was no need for interference at the Essanay studio in Fremont. Directors elsewhere were sometimes cursed for heavy-handed management, but the actors and actresses at Niles had little to complain about. They were able to relax under Billy's informal style and easy approachability. Their ideas and opinions were welcomed by the boss in an atmosphere never poisoned by labor-management bickering.

But it was not so for the nation as a whole. The situation ate at the country's innards until the coming of a genuine leader. When, as president, Theodore Roosevelt was reminded of the ambiguity of constitutional law and the overriding need to go easy on the corporations he fairly sprang upon the offender, grabbed him by both lapels, treated him to a threatening close-up of his famous teeth and fairly shouted, "The Constitution was *made for the people* and *not* the people for the Constitution!" End of conversation. The Leader had arrived.

But the great corporations when at their best, paint another picture. Historian Fraser Harbutt puts it this way: "Yes, the Vanderbilts and Rockefellers were ruthless, but perhaps they served the country well. Admittedly, they crushed the power and culture of old, rural America, but they built a fabulous industrial economy to replace it." Again, on two separate occasions, the "Emperor of Wall Street," J. Pierpont Morgan, head of one of the most powerful banking houses in the world, backed by greater financial strength than many a sovereign country in Europe or the Americas, in control of a third of the country's railroads and two-thirds of its steel production was summoned, or rather respectfully invited, to save the national economy from collapse. The Robber Baron, in working with the White House, supplied a desperate Treasury Department with sixty-two million dollars in gold from his own coffers, twice shoring up Wall Street against the worst effects of economic depression. Rarely, before or since, has the country weathered such a storm in peacetime.

Republican Tom Platt of New York echoed the corporation philosophy when he supported "the right of a man to run his own business in his own way, with due respect of course to the Ten Commandments and the penal code." His gratuitous reference to the Commandments would evoke a wry smile from those whose rights to a business of their own had been unfairly crushed.

These tensions eventuated into a drama between Big Government and Big Business that had to be played out, for America in the 1880s and '90s was embarked upon new and turbulent waters upon which both the ship of state and a contending doctrine of free enterprise were untried. It was clear to all concerned that the country was seriously out of internal balance. It was also clear that the only corrective force that existed was with Congress and the White House.

The antitrust bill, signed into law by President Benjamin Harrison, is so important to our study that it should at this point be subjected to scrutiny. In two brief paragraphs Congress had this to say:

Section One: *Every contract, combination in the form of trust or otherwise, or conspiracy in restraint of trade or commerce among the several States, or with foreign nations, is declared to be illegal. Every person who shall make any contract or engage in any combination or conspiracy hereby declared to be illegal shall be deemed guilty of a felony, and, on conviction thereof shall be punished by fine not exceeding ten million dollars if a corporation, or, if any other person, three hundred and fifty thousand dollars, or by imprisonment not exceeding three years, or by both said punishments, in the discretion of the court.*

Section Two: *Every person who shall monopolize, or attempt to monopolize, or combine or conspire with any other person or persons to monopolize any part of the trade or commerce among the several States, or with foreign nations, shall be deemed guilty of a felony, and on conviction thereof shall be punished by a fine not exceeding ten million dollars if a corporation, or, if any other person, three hundred and fifty thousand dollars, or by imprisonment not exceeding three years, or by both said punishments, in the discretion of the court.*

That was it. Corporate attorneys read it with satisfaction, certain of its impotence, for trained lawyers could see at a glance enough loopholes to stigmatize the Sherman Act as the "Swiss cheese law." The legislators had, perhaps deliberately, failed to define "restraint of trade," "conspiracy," or even "monopoly" to the satisfaction of the courts. Chaotic interpretation persisted for years, and his staff of lawyers comforted Spoor that Essanay could sail on under clear skies for the new law would not be a serious challenge to the Patents Company nor to Essanay.

On the contrary, the Sherman Act was put to use, to the consternation of small businesses and laborers, as a two-edged sword employed not against the great industries but with legal actions against the working man. And the charge against the workers? – the restraint of trade by strikes and picket lines. For a dozen years after its passage, no president invoked the Sherman Act in a labor crisis except to serve an injunction against a union, while the corporations got off unscathed.

Management no longer had to employ thugs to intimidate the workers, for the government now assumed that function, legally. Squadrons of horse-drawn paddy wagons were seen to race into the picket lines where uniformed police with batons would hurl into whomsoever was within reach. Managers could exult as they watched, arms folded, from the big windows of the upper offices.

"Of all forms of tyranny," Roosevelt was later to remark, "the least attractive and the most vulgar is the tyranny of mere wealth, the tyranny of a plutocracy."

This was hardly the advertised intention of the law, and some within the unions, that ineffectual voice for the workers, urged a revival of the terror tactics of the Molly Maguires, that bloody chapter of coal mining history which, to state it once more, the country thought it had outgrown. This state of thinking was brought about by two things: 1) the heavy heel of the capitalists, particularly in Pennsylvania, in grinding down the working man, and 2) the Congress and the courts perceived as apathetic– or worse, as allied to capitalists and ready to endorse their view that what was good for the corporations must be good for the country, that the federal establishment was, in fact, the servant of industry. True enough, according to historian Harold Faulkner, who speaks of "the control of the federal government by the business interests during most of the period after 1860."

Illustrating the depth of the problem a case is on record in which a boy of about ten worked twelve-hour days in the mines at forty cents a day, with management appropriating the entire pitiable amount to pay off a bill at the company store incurred by his father, who had perished in a mining accident four years earlier.

Sad to say, George K. Spoor, a good and decent person, was a partaker of the prevailing philosophy. He seemed oblivious to the gathering clouds after Roosevelt was in power as, for one corporation after another, the White House acted with determination and great corporations were broken up into their component parts. And it was the ambiguous Sherman Antitrust Act that put into Roosevelt's hands the big stick for which he became notorious.

10

Settling into Niles

Returning to our story, Anderson and his crew settled down in Fremont's Niles district, which he was intending as a permanent location for Essanay. And with that, he made himself thoroughly at home, too much so according to Charlie Chaplin, who arrived there in 1915 and described the pigpen he found when Anderson led him, slightly aghast, into his bachelor quarters near the studio. What a mess! Even though he was then making $125,000 a year and was a millionaire in the days before he could be taxed, Billy kept his cottage, which was neat enough on the outside, virtually unfurnished except for a cot, a small table, one chair and a few ashtrays. The stink of stale tobacco and litter decorating the unswept floor offended visitors like the fastidious Chaplin.

Ah, but this is the one point upon which Broncho Billy may be compared with Ludwig Van Beethoven (admittedly a weird comparison), for both men were able to drive a housekeeper to distraction, preferring to be judged only by the quality of their work. Chaplin however, an admirer of Beethoven, would surely never stomach any comparison of the two.

Billy spent most of his free time in San Francisco, but even there he preferred the smaller, inexpensive hotels. Eccentric (in this case a euphemism for "cheapskate") is a fair word for it, although in the theatrical world from the days of the ancient Greeks, eccentricity has been the norm.

Anderson had a wife, a charming woman according to Chaplin (apparently, he had met the family) and a daughter who lived in luxurious circumstances in Chicago, but he rarely saw either of them. No exemplar as a husband or a father, Gilbert Anderson might have profited from the lessons of his own Broncho Billy films. But the details of that story went to the grave with each of the family members.

In this we see the celebrated sins of show business visible from the earliest years. Screen performers are rarely Oscar nominees in the family-values category for their off-screen roles. Fremont resident Betty Hannah, as witness to some of it, phrased it neatly that "The entertainment world never lost its virtue because it could not lose something that it never had to begin with." And our hero was no better nor worse than the common run of them.

To illustrate, a sweet young thing living in Niles, one Edna Sharp, having caught the movie star virus, straightened her skirt, arranged her hair just so, and approached Anderson to offer her talents as an actress. The lecher lurking within revealed itself as he cast an appraising eye over her, turned her this way and that, then suggested a way whereby she might improve her chances for a career. Her sensitivities properly outraged, Edna turned on her heel and strode out of his presence vowing never to return, resolved upon a less demanding profession.

The two came into contact, or rather into collision, on a later occasion in the dining room of the Belvoir Hotel. Virginia Swanson remembers it as a well-appointed eatery with tablecloths and napkins of fine linen rather than paper, as close to "class'" as one could expect south of Oakland. The owner had a bevy of attractive daughters, including Edna, who would frequently grace the premises by waiting on tables. One day after work Anderson sashayed in, found an empty table and sat down, requesting a menu which was duly placed before him. Scowling as he saw ham on the main course, he allowed his boorish streak to erupt as he swore, flung down his napkin and exclaimed, "You know I can't eat ham!" Edna remarked quietly and yet loud enough to be heard, "Why Mr. Anderson, I thought you were Scandinavian." This was too much for the movie magnate who stormed out vowing never to return, much to the relief of the giggling Belvoir staff.

These vignettes were not uncommon, although they never threatened the overall stability of the relationship between the town and the studio. There long remained with Marie Bishop, Mary Clute and other residents

CHAPTER 10: SETTLING INTO NILES

a recognition of Anderson's stature as an actor and director, but they coupled it with observations such as "emotionally unstable," "odd," and "erratic," which detract from his afterglow. "And he could have a vile temper when he wanted to," According to Jim Wilson. These were their opinions not just of Broncho Billy, but of the whole business. "We sort of turned up our noses at actors then," sniffed one elderly matron. "They were a little different. How would you say it? – not of good character. They wore flashy clothes, had flashy cars. You knew right away, there goes an actor."

Anderson's wealth of mouth sometimes got him into hot water with his people, for his actors could be just as set in their ways as were the townspeople. Marie Dressler was a comedienne of hefty proportions with a successful 1914 debut in *Tillie's Punctured Romance,* a six-reel Chaplin comedy, followed by two more "Tillies" the following year. It had promise of becoming a series. Once while managing a picture and trying to manage Marie, Billy managed instead to get his kisser smacked by the actress who stormed out vowing never to return. "She knocked him on his ___," says old-time resident Art Fereira with a grin. The cause of the dustup has been long forgotten; presumably Billy suggested a way whereby she might improve her chances for a career.

But among others who knew him a happier side comes through. Chaplin liked Billy and speaks of "a special kind of charm." Early in their acquaintance and before Chaplin had reached the top of his form, Anderson had taken the kind of interest in him that might be expected of a big brother, a solicitude that ripened into mutual respect.

Also ripening was the attitude of Fremont residents toward this new phenomenon with the largest buildings in the business district. Prior to 1913 when Essanay swung into high gear with its handsome new block-long studio at First and G streets, there was nary a word in the local paper about current movies, and rarely about entertainment of any kind.

Back then there were "movie circuits" to serve the smaller communities. Theater chains, based in the cities, would send out one or two men with a projector to set up shop in an empty building or a barn, collect some loose change, show their film, then move on to the next town, this perhaps on a weekly basis. But now, with a movie studio as a local presence, those touring technicians were no longer necessary. The *Washington Press* could announce: "Edison Moving Pictures Company shows in Irvington every Wednesday and Saturday night," on a routine basis, and all five hamlets which were later organized into the city of Fremont were thenceforth treated to an increasing volume of film entertainment.

The presence of the studio soon changed quiet evenings by the fireplace into an abundance of comedies, dramas and shoot 'em ups every night and all over the place. On July 12, 1913, thirty-three lines of newspaper column space listed the pictures for the coming week. On August 2 this had risen to 54, and by January 3, 1914, sixty-eight. This pedantic routine of reading each issue and counting lines is the worst form of drudgery, and yet it proved useful by revealing Fremont's heartbeat as the country maid fell increasingly in love with the city slicker. By February the paper was devoting seventy lines to current movies, abnormal coverage for a mere village, and by May of 1914, a whopping ninety lines exceeded that given to movies by the *Oakland Tribune* or the *San Francisco Chronicle*. The *Washington Press*, moreover, with every appearance of true love, maintained that degree of coverage for as long as the studio was turning out its ever-popular comedies and Westerns.

From a standing start of total apathy in 1912, the Fremont area in less than two years had become movie-oriented with a vengeance. And while Broncho Billy and his "Snakeville Boys" were shooting pictures, careening down the dusty streets in stage coaches, gunfire intruding into every private conversation, it was impossible to ignore what was going on at First and G.

CHAPTER 10: SETTLING INTO NILES

Midmorning it is, around ten o'clock, and the sun is high enough to make the camera crews, three or four of them, anticipate a great day. Ben Turpin with two or three others and with his own cameraman cranking away, would be at work on a comedy and in a world of their own. Anderson had been up most of the night on the script, let us say, for a movie to be called *Broncho Billy's Word of Honor*. He usually put his stories together during the quiet of the night to be ready for filming the next day, for processing in the lab that afternoon, then whisked back to Chicago on the next train. How nice it was to have the train station just across the street from the studio. Union Pacific found it advisable to stop at Fremont, says Harry Avila, more frequently than it had before Essanay moved in.

Jim Wilson remembers that the horses would be led out of their stalls two and three at a time, frisking and pawing the ground, and that some of the kids could be expected to skip school on such a day, another headache for parents whose worries about theatrical temptations were thereby reinforced. Billy would be everywhere at once sending the camera crews in different directions and giving a few cowboys the first and only briefing they would get, or would need. Rarely did they have to shoot a retake in the days before sound.

Lila Hunt tells us that there was an old cabin a few blocks from the main studio that had been turned over to Essanay and that Billy had directed his camera people to tear off its roof to allow a flood of sunlight. This was necessary for the indoor shots. Edison had yet to come up with film quality that would do justice to shadowy scenes. Clusters of townspeople would form on the clapboard sidewalks or peer from windows, delighted to serve as atmosphere if asked. Some, in fact, would come for just that, waiting off to one side and hoping for Anderson to beckon a few of them to stand over here or there, which they would scurry to do. Some, no doubt, entertained visions high and mighty of what their next step up the ladder to stardom would be, only to be told "Okay, that's all; you can go home now." But even so, the studio had delivered on its promise and everybody had enjoyed a good time.

Among the earliest signs of change was a brief notice in the *Washington*

Press dated March 14, 1913, announcing that the Edison Company planned to build a local theater only for movies. Commonplace today, it was an innovation back then. And the new theater would have a seating capacity (400) which would accommodate the entire town. The ambitious picture program in the same issue tells why. Vitagraph was featuring four films that week, Biograph two, Kalem three, Selig one, Essanay five, Edison one, and Lubin two, and all of it in the Fremont area. One may wonder if, by that time, watching movies had become the only leisure activity. Whatever had happened to checkers and horseshoes?

The five films from Essanay included three Broncho Billies: *The Man in the Cabin, Broncho Billy's Conscience,* and *A Western Sister's Devotion,* plus two comedies: *The Accidental Bandit* and *Alkali Ike's Gal,* with Gus Carney. This comedian, Augustus Carney, had achieved some status on the Essanay lot for he had the freedom to requisition any cowboy or cameraman that wasn't doing something else. And with his *ad hoc* arrangement he cranked out his own series of *Alkali Ikes*. Carney had built up a loyal following among theater-goers but nothing that was produced in Fremont ever achieved the popularity of Billy's Westerns.

With one possible exception. Early in 1915 Anderson, with a nod of assent from the Chicago office, welcomed into the Fremont studio a rising new comedian named Charlie Chaplin. Anderson signed him up to make fifteen films for Essanay.

11

Enter Charlie Chaplin

"A day without laughter is a day wasted. Failure is unimportant. It takes courage to make a fool of yourself."

—Charlie Chaplin

It was one sweetheart deal whereby the new star was granted a series of freedoms tailored to his every whim and beginning, as we have seen, with a salary that was the wonder of the entertainment world. Moreover, he was permitted to write and direct his own pictures with virtually no oversight.

Comedians in every age have been dime-a-dozen people on the lowest rung of the theatrical ladder. Specialists in foolishness they have always been, and to regard their film contributions in that early era as an "art form" would have been laughable. In virtually every studio, directors regarded comedians as easy-to-replace and low-paid employees.

When, therefore, a genuine artist did stand before the cameras, directors and producers, the lot of them, reacted in a predictable pattern and contrary to their own best interests. Charles Spencer Chaplin, comedian, was held in the customary low regard.

For years Chaplin had been among those actors who had chafed under what has been earlier referred to as micro-management. But the artistry within him simply could not flower under a repressive boss who, in front of others and before the cameras, would bark at him, telling him how to do that which he had under perfect control.

Director Mack Sennett at the Keystone studio really got under his skin. Sennett was a puppeteer who generally had a marvelous feel for antics that would bring down the house, and his Keystone Kop sequences, hilarious even yet, bear witness to this. But as a director, he was a pain.

Chaplin parted company with him for two reasons. He was drawn *to* Essanay by a well-baited hook, and he was driven *from* Keystone by a relationship gone sour. But such was his strength at the box office that he suffered no loss by getting Sennett off his case. Chaplin was no puppet.

His experience at Keystone confirmed the actor in henceforth directing his own productions. "Artistic license" he called it, and he demanded it for the whole of his long career. Anderson found it easy to write this provision into Chaplin's contract for it was a concept that he could relate to; it had been Broncho Billy's own guiding star for years and at the heart of the success of his western films.

* * * * *

Of his fifteen contracted films, the first was made at the Chicago studio, five at Fremont, and for those remaining Chaplin broke away to a better equipped Essanay branch at Los Angeles. Among the senior citizens living in Fremont today, the few who have not yet been gathered unto their fathers, much is made of those few weeks that Chaplin spent in Niles. When he arrived he still had some growing to do, but by the time he left he had arrived at artistic maturity. Fremont residents Amelia Silva and Jim Wilson agreed that the town still feels honored to have had him there for an important part of his early career.

Screen historians have contributed almost nothing to our appreciation of Chaplin's experience in Fremont. Some would apparently have us believe that this actor's success imparted a measure of glory to whatever studios he happened to work with, but this was surely not the case with his brief interlude at Essanay. There the balance was the other way around, as Art Fereira insists, for it was Anderson and Essanay and the village of Niles in Fremont that extended to the comedian a degree of professional respect that he was never accorded in his previous experience.

Chaplin was, at Essanay, the recipient of a golden opportunity at a time when he needed it. It was in those five pictures at Niles, especially

CHAPTER 11: ENTER CHARLIE CHAPLIN

the fifth which the world knows as *The Tramp*, that Chaplin emerged from his cocoon as a mere comedian and into something like maturity as a dramatic actor.

Considering the scores of films great and small that Chaplin has made, *The Tramp* is the one for which he is most renowned. Sound and color notwithstanding, his subsequent productions never approached it, and the case can easily be made that without the now-extinct Essanay Company and the town where it nested, *The Tramp* would never have seen the light of day. Chaplin's professional indebtedness to Fremont is profound.

But this gets ahead of our story. Let's go back a bit to when Billy and Charlie first came to know each other. It is one of the most curious and convoluted tales in entertainment history, and not without numerous episodes of comic relief.

Chaplin's first awareness of Essanay came, as we have seen, as he was growing disenchanted with his situation at Keystone. He had worked there for about a year and by 1914 had made thirty-five films, including one feature. Although rudimentary and with seldom anything like a storyline (improvisation before the camera was the thing to do) Chaplin's work, like Anderson's was an essay into the unknown.

By far his most important accomplishment while with Sennett was his stroke of genius at combining the derby, baggy trousers, oversized shoes and specific type of cane into the accouterments later made so famous at Essanay. And it was an odd lapse of judgment by which Sennett allowed it to all slip through his fingers.

Public response, which is to say the bottom line, was what mattered and public response to Chaplin, despite Sennett's relative inattention to him, was becoming phenomenal. It was to the actor's popularity that the Fremont branch of Essanay was paying very close attention.

One day Chaplin awoke to discover that he was making peanuts for himself at $125 a week and a fortune for the Keystone Studio, and to his angry dismay the front office was content to leave matters as they stood. Sennett was becoming dimly aware that the biggest money-maker he had ever latched onto was discontented. He had enough sense to do something about it, but not enough to do the right thing.

He quietly ordered all approaches to Chaplin guarded and strangers shooed away from the Keystone lot, but this did not prevent counter-intrigue by an Essanay secret agent who disguised himself as a cowboy extra, snuck onto the premises, located the comedian when nobody else was within earshot, and surreptitiously slipped to Chaplin a mouthwatering menu featuring a main course equal to ten times his present salary, or $1,250 a week, a fantastic amount, and for dessert, a $10,000 immediate bonus. Then Sennett, a veteran pie-throwing enthusiast, put up a real battle by countering Essanay's $1,250 with a magnanimously inequitable counteroffer of $750, plus no dessert.

On such fare Chaplin would lose weight. What on earth was Sennett thinking about? It was for things like this that historian Gerald Mast called him "chintzy." In any case Chaplin did not have to consider Anderson's offer for more than a moment before tucking a napkin under his chin.

But the far-sighted Anderson had arranged this on his own authority and of course had to confirm it with the shortsighted George Spoor. And when Chicago got wind of Chaplin's gold-plated contract, Spoor hit the ceiling. His best comedians were being paid $75 a week with no nonsense over bonuses or who would do the directing.

Anderson was feeling sure of his judgment on this, but clearly there was only one thing to do. Chaplin must get himself to the central office posthaste and personally meet with Godzilla. Accordingly this was arranged.

The actor was next on his way to meet the man who held the cash register keys and by virtue of his personality attempt to smooth out the wrinkles. George Spoor was aware that Chaplin was scheduled to meet with him, that the ball was in his court and that time was short. For this, he had a classic non-solution: he got out of town.

For weeks the boss made himself scarce while he mulled the matter over. Chaplin, knowing that Spoor could not absent himself from his studio forever, pulled up a chair, made himself at home and waited. Day in and day out, he sat in the office and waited.

CHAPTER 11: ENTER CHARLIE CHAPLIN

The matter was settled in the best comic-opera tradition when Spoor had a brainstorm that tested Anderson's insistence that Chaplin was well worth the money. With nothing better to do than to sit in a hotel lobby and think, Spoor had Chaplin paged while he stood by to watch people's reaction. The name Chaplin, called in a loud voice, was electric. Nearly everybody left whatever he was doing to follow the bellhop, hoping for a glimpse of the celebrity.

That did it; Spoor was convinced. He breezed back to the Windy City, all smiles, and signed everything. The relieved Chaplin got his contract, his bonus and an apology: "Sorry for the delay, business matters, you know." On January 2, 1915, it was announced to the newspapers that this rising star was now working for the energetic Essanay firm for an obscene amount of money.

> *"I went into the business for the money and the art grew out of it. If people are disillusioned by that remark, I can't help it. It's the truth."*
> Charlie Chaplin

One detail remained. Just as Edwin S. Porter had earlier screen tested Anderson, so did Spoor ease his own mind concerning this very expensive new acquisition, Charlie Chaplin. While still in Chicago, the actor was politely invited to make a picture while Spoor sat back to be entertained. Chaplin was allowed some open space, a few supporting actors and a camera crew and immediately set to work. Anderson had to wait while the studio produced, on the first of February, Charlie's first Essanay comedy, a two-reeler aptly entitled *His New Job*. It was his usual impromptu series of antics with no rehearsal, no script, hardly any setting, just whatever the actor found lying around the studio. With impressive flexibility, low-budget Chaplin was becoming very good at creating something from virtually nothing. Chaplin and a chair, or Chaplin and an umbrella, or Chaplin and a lamp post; he needed nothing more. Richard Attenborough's 1992 biographical film, *Chaplin,* although replete with errors, caught Chaplin's spirit by having him say: "Sometimes I feel so close to getting it right." This is the spirit of artistry.

Having seen his new "employee" in action, Spoor was satisfied and

Anderson was free to introduce him to the Essanay lot in Northern California. Wondering what, if any, civilized amenities the semi-developed West had to offer, Chaplin was induced to make the trip into the spaces around wild and woolly Fremont.

12

Chaos in the Streets

The differences between motion pictures prior to 1915 and now are vast. At that time the term "stardom" was not in the vocabulary; there were only employees at the bottom of the food chain. Nor was there any of the glamour we see today, no handprints in the cement, no Champagne poured from a slipper. Film acting was not yet a profession, certainly not an art; it was a minor industry and a mere job with the "actors" spending as much time behind a broom as before a camera. Fifty cents an hour was the going rate of pay, nothing to write home about.

It took about another decade for the term "movie star" to become current. It was Chaplin (and Mary Pickford, who by 1915, was making $10,000 a week) who broke the ice, making life easier for the actors who came later. Name recognition with the public was a hard uphill battle against management. Broadway stage performers had no problem with this for theirs was a tradition going back to Shakespeare, and personal renown with their names emblazoned had long been their reward.

But acting before a camera was still a novelty. It began as minimum-wage servitude, although film actors could see no essential difference between stage and screen. And they were keenly sensitive about being shoved into anonymity by producers who had no objection to profiteering at their expense. In those halcyon days before the introduction of the IRS, producers living in opulence were not about to retreat an inch, honoring an unwritten agreement among themselves to keep "employees" strictly subordinate. Their overriding fear was that an actor eyeing Chaplin as a role model would demand an ever-higher salary, and this could come only from the coffers of the producer. It was this stonewalling by management that eventually forced actors to unionize, and that put a whole new face on things. As for Anderson, he moved easily between both camps. Having begun with minor parts, and perhaps a broom and dust pan in supporting roles, he was capable also of managing a large operation, and in any case was never accused of divided loyalties. His career moved easily from one side of the line to the other and prospered under both flags.

Inventions and improvements upon them came thick and fast. Edison's kinetoscope had been revealed to a wide-eyed New York audience back in April of 1894. In the previous year, the French had weighed in with something called a cine-camera, or cinematograph, developed by August and Louis Lumiere, but this had to await Edison's refinements before it was really workable.

Those far-seeing gentlemen, the brothers Lumiere, are a fascinating study of the innovative approach. Chemists by profession, they came out in 1895 with the first genuine movie, *La Sortie des Usines Lumiere,* or "Workers Leaving the Lumiere Factory," not much of a storyline but something. They were the first to produce newsreels, and as early as 1903 startled the entertainment world with experimental photographs in color. Edison took careful notice, for the gentlemen were thinking light years ahead of the times.

It must be added that had it not been for the genius and business drive of Thomas Alva Edison our country would have been dependent from the beginning upon European initiative in all areas of photography, including motion pictures. And of all Edison's competitors the French were the sharpest.

· · · · ·

Roaming the streets of the old Niles district, this writer listened to many a resident such as Wilhemina Berge and Ellen Cornish, at that time only children, tell of how their parents often yearned for the good old days when nothing much ever happened. Discontent was especially rife during the early weeks of the "takeover." Before the initial shock had worn off, the townspeople had become fed up with stepping over horse manure, with high-toned women, with cowboys spitting tobacco juice and with actors as well as actresses behind too much lipstick. How disgusting. (Old-fashioned townspeople had to be patiently educated that in some scenes the hero's lips were hardly visible; therefore lipstick to accentuate his masculinity.) Often there was noise everywhere, augmented by shouting and gunfire, and there seemed no way to escape it. Traffic control was nonexistent except when Anderson posted his own staff to warn people away. Whether it was a posse in pursuit of varmints or a stagecoach laden with the payroll, the movies took control of the streets, pushing everybody out of camera range while stirring up clouds of choking dust. The center of town no longer belonged to the people.

During those opening weeks, singly and in groups, townsfolk would walk up to the man in shirtsleeves who was obviously in charge of this circus to complain that the disruption was turning their lives upside down. Anderson, at this stage realizing his dependence upon everyone's good will, would stop whatever he was doing to explain that his crew was creating a new entertainment form and in the process would solve the town's problems. That was important, and he was sure to emphasize it. The town fathers rejoined that they had no problems, until now that is. Give us a little time, Anderson would plead, and watch what happens.

The studio really needed the town; it needed help of all sorts and relied upon goodhearted souls to make themselves useful, which they would do just to have a part in the enterprise. Anderson went out of his way to cultivate good relations and urged his people to do the same. As a result, Essanay saved a bundle on free services. And when the company did pay, it paid well,, with openings for carpenters, blacksmiths, horse groomers, pick-and-shovel men, and as a treat an occasional chance to appear onscreen. Their smiling faces, they were informed, would be seen in New York, in Europe, even in China. That must have been something to boast about.

Groups might be needed to simply stand in the background as atmosphere, which the people would do for no pay. Moreover, the "trickle-down theory" was at work in that payroll money sent from the Chicago office for the regular staff soon fertilized the whole community. Liquid assets of local businesses, thanks to the studio, within a couple of months of Essanay's arrival began a water-to-wine transformation and for the first time ever, cash began to flow in Niles.

Anderson's promise of solutions was thus fulfilled. More than that, the big industry squeezed tightly into the town also provided the problems that had been previously lacking, so that in time everybody was satisfied.

The town and the studio had arrived at a healthy working relationship, and Fremont was on its way to becoming the centerpiece of the motion picture industry in America. That surely gave the citizens a sense of pride. By 1912 the industry down south was in the early stages of carving out an empire based in Hollywood, but it was in Fremont that Hollywood's only serious competition was to be found. The Essanay Company's Northern California branch in the brief span of four years was setting precedents that the later Hollywood moguls would be pleased to capitalize on.

Chaplin wasted no time. His first picture in Fremont, *His Night Out*, came only a few days after he had unpacked his suitcases in a small but comfortable bungalow, still standing and still occupied, across the street from the studio. It's a safe bet that he kept it a good deal neater than Broncho Billy kept his. So well organized was he that he had already found the leading lady who would remain with him until 1923. Edna Purviance, then 19, was wasting away as a waitress at Tate's Café on Hill Street in San Francisco when she was "discovered" by Essanay cowboy, Carl Strauss, who had been sent by Chaplin with that specific mission. The details of her written contract are unknown, but we can safely guess at what the verbal arrangements must have been. For the ensuing eight years she appeared in all but two of his pictures, as well as an unknowable number of his private, off-camera carnal endeavors. Again, Chaplin wasted no time.

Lost to memory now are the names and faces of his supporting cast at Fremont: Fred Goodwin, Ben Turpin and Leo White. On March 11, *The Champion* was sent to Chicago where it made the rounds of theaters. In this one, Anderson left his Westerns long enough to serve as an extra. *In the Park* came exactly a week later, followed by *A Jitney Elopement*, "jitney" being the old-fashioned name for an automobile. In these four films, the cast of characters was always the same, perhaps with the addition of Lloyd Bacon or Paddy McGuire.

The Tramp, and the Road Never Taken

On the heels of these came Chaplin's classic *The Tramp*, on April 11, 1915. Filmed in the unspoiled and still picturesque Niles Canyon, it established Chaplin's trademark as the pathetic little loser in baggy pants trudging off down a dusty road. With this film he reached his pinnacle of artistic success. The subsequent march of time witnessed fabulous advances in film technology, in sound, then in color and much else, but it was this simplistic production in black and white that some critics still believe capped his career.

But to keep our balance, it must be added that a viewer today sitting back to watch *The Tramp* will have trouble applying the word "classic" to it. The opening scene is of Chaplin walking down a wooded country lane toward the camera. The film closes with Chaplin walking down the same country lane *away* from the camera. All else is of the same genre of slapstick comedy that marked every previous and every subsequent production. As mentioned earlier, however, audiences in 1915 lacked the sophistication that is commonplace among us today, and to some degree this may explain its enthusiastic reception.

But upon reflection, that may be a self-serving judgment, implying that people then were somehow less intelligent than today's box-office crowd. On the contrary, our great-grandparents kept pace with every innovation, and moreover developed a shrewdness at interpreting the obscure message of a film where there was no verbalization to convey it, a skill not easy for us moderns to attain. In this writer's experience with silent films, it has sometimes been necessary to view a sequence again and again, before the nuances of body language and facial expression become intelligible. Only thus may a person bridge what amounts to a minor cultural gap between past and present, and then the storyline of an ancient movie may be rightly understood. What this means is that it may be *our* generation that lacks the sophistication that was once commonplace; the "talkies" made such a talent unnecessary, so it atrophied. For everything gained there is something lost, and the quality we call sophistication merely changes in shape from one age to another.

In any case, Chaplin's fans were delighted with the film, the movie circuits were demanding it, and George Spoor was rubbing his hands in glee.

After that picture, his work at the Fremont studio was history. Glad to be out of there, the little winner in baggy pants and pockets filled with cash turned his shuffling gait southward. He never returned. On the 29th of April, two weeks after the release of *The Tramp*, he arrived at a new Essanay studio in Los Angeles to finish out his contract.

Although he had been at Fremont for less than three months, he had succeeded beyond his wildest dreams at Keystone. His imprint upon the city is now faded beyond recall, having died with the generation that knew him, but what Niles Canyon had done for Charlie Chaplin kept its luster throughout his life. His subsequent experience in Hollywood did little more than build upon the foundation he had already established while at Fremont.

With all this, one is disappointed to learn that his brief stay there was not a happy time. From the moment he got off the train, Chaplin didn't like the place. There was nothing there for him. But the town made efforts to welcome him, even to overlooking his obvious hanky-panky with his

CHAPTER 13: THE TRAMP, AND THE ROAD NEVER TAKEN

leading lady, scandalous in a conservative community. At no time did the local newspaper breathe a word of Charlie and Edna quartered in the same Essanay cottage. Nevertheless, Charlie's gaze was increasingly fixed upon the new studios then springing up around Los Angeles. He had grown accustomed to being courted by executives trying to throw money his way. It was up the ladder for him, and he was prepared to sell his vivid persona to the highest bidder.

And besides, what was there to do in a small town when one was through for the day except sit on a haystack and read a book? Or relax on a hilltop and count the passing cars? (Four or five a day was about average; Los Angeles had somewhat more.)

Anderson sympathized with Chaplin, for although Broncho Billy needed the town, Anderson got away as often as he could for refreshment in San Francisco. His own roots in Niles remained shallow. His alter ego was a movie cowboy in need of a Western setting, but Chaplin's career for all its success was painfully one-dimensional. He had his eye on wealth and the Big City, and this meant a night life without frogs or crickets. And what could the county maid say to this?

Spoor had permitted Anderson to take Chaplin to the Niles studio, trusting that the actor would find ample scope there for his talents, which of course he did. But unlike the more congenial Ben Turpin, who enjoyed a fine relationship with the townspeople, Chaplin chose to remain aloof from almost everybody. Lila Hunt, Art Fereira and others remember him now not for his comical films but for his chilly, impersonal demeanor. For a while he roomed at the Wesley at First and H Streets, often eating at the Belvoir where he neglected to tip the waitresses. One old timer recalls that Chaplin used to drop by his grocery store and help himself to free walnuts. Gossip had it that he would sponge free billiard games off Anderson over at Billy Moore's saloon. Trivial scratches all, that would have vanished from memory had Chaplin's natural humor expressed itself in acts of common courtesy, but that seldom happened. The old-time residents consulted by this writer agree with Art Fereira, who reminisces poetically, "That SOB ever did anything for this town."

Even in later years, Chaplin had not mellowed, nor could he even assume a friendlier posture for old time's sake. More recently, when he had been honored by the Queen of England, Fremont sent a telegram of congratulations and invited his return to Niles to dedicate a unique museum, then in the planning stage and to be named in his honor. Chaplin did not even trouble himself to reply.

This was unfortunate for a number of reasons, a few of which concern us here. Had he been gracious enough to appear, even by proxy, the museum idea would have taken off. It might have existed to this day and heaven only knows the artifacts and memorabilia, the private letters of the stars and collectibles accumulating year by year, that would be preserved for all to enjoy. Attached to the museum one may envision a small movie theater specializing in antique films, to which would be added a library of century-old books and manuscripts to make Fremont a diamond mine for school kids and serious historians alike. Such a museum and such a library collection with proper management could have won the respect of the Bancroft Library, the university in Hayward, and have gone far to put Fremont on the intellectual map.

But this road was never taken, and a sorry lapse of discernment it was on the part of Mr. Chaplin. Did his star-gazing at Tinsel Town preoccupied him so thoroughly that he abandoned Niles? Worse, following Chaplin's lead, an entire generation of competent researchers have managed to ignore Fremont's four years of contributions to the motion picture field. The celebrated actor steered his biographers away from his Nile's experience and those writers respected his wishes. But they carried it too far, apparently in the mistaken notion that Chaplin was the only actor of true worth to come out of the Niles studio, and that is surely not the case. The earliest writers produced the source material presently on library shelves. This material has been utilized by authors who followed, and thus the problem has perpetuated itself. The result has been that an important bloc of motion picture history to this day has never had an investigative light thrown into it.

There were two great centers of motion picture production in the American West. The one that has concerned us here was ultimately overridden by what transpired in Hollywood. Our appreciation of motion

CHAPTER 13: THE TRAMP, AND THE ROAD NEVER TAKEN

picture history is inadequate if we fail to account for the advances pioneered by the studio in Fremont, a fleeting four years, but with a legacy still discernible after nearly a century.

But to continue, the studio went all out to keep its touchy star contented. At one time Chaplin was tempted to receive a $25,000 offer for two weeks of fifteen-minute appearances at the New York Hippodrome. He was on the verge of absenting himself from Essanay just long enough to reap this easy harvest when Anderson came across with the full amount just to keep him where he was.

By 1915, toys and statuettes of the comedian were on display in stores across the land. Fan clubs were mushrooming all over, and his mail was becoming a burden to the local post office. Chaplin's life appeared to be made of notoriety, Champagne and money.

His half-brother Sydney did some basic math, and then set before him some startling figures. By his calculations it was obvious that if Chaplin's pictures were marketed at a rate that coincided with the size of the theater, each film might bring in over $100,000. Upon this revelation, Chaplin let it be known that he was being underpaid, according to the original terms of his contract.

At this time, as Anderson was aware, Chaplin had produced only five short films for Essanay in addition to *The Tramp*, but such was his popularity that even this slight output had garnered a total of $1.3 million, not bad for films each of which had cost only $1,200 to $1,500 to make. Broncho Billy's cowboy pictures could not do nearly as well, so Anderson did the smart thing: He rewrote Chaplin's contract.

Billy set an offer on the table of a $100,000 bonus for each film in addition to $350,000 for a dozen two-reelers. Chaplin accepted, and the two men shook hands on the deal.

14

A Vivid American Cultural Scene

By this time, 1915, the city slicker and the country maid had become closely intertwined in a relationship producing many a sweet blossom. But Broncho Billy had his hands full riding herd on the crew in addition to turning out cowboy films at an undiminished rate. As a result he was never able to serve on the chamber of commerce nor take part in civic affairs.

Not so with his actors, however, many of whom barged whole-heartedly into the life of the village and cultivated warm friendships.

Victor Potel, a popular comedian better known as Slippery Slim, was especially well-liked. His marriage on November 23, 1914 was a cork-popper that enlivened Billy Moore's saloon, the front page of the *Register* and several square blocks as the town rejoiced with him.

A few of those magnificent mediocrities clawed their way above the herd with personal followings of their own, forging ahead to genuine stardom. Ben Turpin and Wallace Beery were among them; their names retaining a luster long after the old Essanay buildings had been bulldozed into mere memory.

Ben Turpin was a lovable, popular cross-eyed comic who always had a good word for whomever he met. Wallace Beery was another winner, with a marvelous future in both comedy and drama. Turpin was before the time of this writer, but Beery is still unforgettable as the caustic Foreign Legion sergeant in *Beau Geste*, as well as a star in a comedy series with Marjory Main. Much later, in 1934, he starred in *Viva Villa*, a film that "…revealed comedian Wallace Beery for the great actor he was," wrote

Richard Griffith and Arthur Mayer in 1970. But it was as a comic star that the young tough was broken in on the Essanay lot.

In his Fremont days, Beery was often like a rebellious teenager. With enough money saved to buy a new Turner runabout, the main street in Niles became his race track. And as with galloping horses, mothers again had to clutch their children close to them when Beery came flying down the street. "I had the darndest time keeping him out of jail," complained Leon Solon, the Niles traffic cop. On one occasion, he managed to elude a posse of police cars chasing him from San Jose. But they had his license number, and may also have known him by reputation, serving him later with a warrant. Bail was set at two hundred dollars, a remarkable sum at that time for a traffic violation, which Beery decided to forfeit rather than face a judge.

Ben Turpin was also pulled in once, both he and Anderson, by Constable Frank Rose as they splashed around like kids in a Niles Canyon pool chasing wild ducks in violation of the game law. Harmless antics.

The generation that can remember Ben Turpin has long passed from the scene, but he used to be remembered for his hilarity in jumping off buildings, being dunked in the horse troughs, and posing as "September Morn" in local parades. Years later in 1934, when the ex-policeman Solon had opened a service station on the old studio site, good-natured Ben actually made the trip all the way from Hollywood to pump gas and attract business for his friend who later commented, "There are people who will never get over having their windshields wiped by that crazy guy with the crossed eyes."

Chaplin and Turpin were two famed professionals working for the same studio in the same town and sometimes in the same pictures. One loved the place, the other couldn't stand it. Perhaps Turpin had the better right to complain, for he was paid only $25 a week while watching Chaplin receive $1,250.

But we must spend more time with Turpin and Chaplin, especially in their early, formative years, if a fair comparison is to be made.

The details in the life of Charles Chaplin can be very hard to pin down, so contradictory and unreliable are the sources, including his

CHAPTER 14: A VIVID AMERICAN CULTURAL SCENE

own autobiography, which almost certainly had been given over to a ghostwriter. But the main outline is clear enough and agreed upon all around. That outline tells us this: that Chaplin's early life in the London slums was an ordeal that no child should have to live through. Concerned people at the close of the twentieth century who drum into our ears, as well they should, the horrors of inner-city life have inherited their mission, their uphill struggle against urban poverty, from the century's beginning. "The poor ye always have with you," we read in the book of Matthew. Chaplin's childhood, skipped over in his autobiography to the point of a whitewash, is a commentary on that verse and could well have filled a page or two in the 1903 work by Jack London, *People of the Abyss*.

Chaplin was born in 1889 at a time when the London Congregational Union had raised a howl of popular outrage against the plight of the poor with its publication of *The Bitter Cry*, describing the wretched existence of humans in Liverpool and London, surely including the family garret on Pownall Terrace, who would have been happier had they never been born. The ancient philosopher Plato agreed with Jack London when he stated, "Any ordinary city is in fact two cities, one the city of the poor, the other the rich, each at war with the other."

If Charlie as a boy had not been actually homeless it was because his otherwise loving mother, Hannah, had so frequently sold herself into prostitution to prevent it, and to keep he and his brother Sidney from utter starvation. Lack of nourishment, in fact, may have kept Charlie from growing beyond five feet four, and he was always slight of build. The "home" that Hannah was able to provide for her fatherless boys was usually that eight-foot square cubicle on Pownall Terrace, further cramped by the slanted attic roof, complete with dirt, a broken-down cot, an upturned box for a table, and a population of large rats sufficiently vicious to deprive an unguarded infant of his fingers, toes and face. He reminisces about "the wretchedness of our garret," no theatrical fabrication but a plain description of the squalor that Chaplin as a boy had witnessed all around him.

Sidney (later to be spelled Sydney), four years his senior, looked after Charlie while their mother, in spite of striving hard to be a Christian woman, was working at a profession that, coupled with alcoholism and abject poverty, ultimately drove her out of her mind.

And yet there remained to them a genuine, shared devotion that bound the mother to her sons, a truth that shines in Chaplin's own commentary and is well-attested in other sources. Her own lot would have been improved if, as many a woman had done, she had simply abandoned the boys, but she would not entertain such a solution. She tried to support the family with her sewing machine, slaving through the wee hours of the morning stitching little things on consignment from a nearby outlet. But she could not keep up with it and the quality of her work suffered. "I never realized," wrote Charlie years later, "that she was weak from malnutrition." A disaster it was for the mother and her sons when she fell behind in the payments and the precious sewing machine was repossessed.

Hannah was a singer and stage performer, dainty and quite pretty but essentially untrained, from whom Charlie as a child learned the rudiments of singing and dancing to the applause of working-class crowds that showered him with coins. It was this that told the mother that her son had a talent that should be nurtured. She agreed, albeit with regret, that her young teenager go for a time with a popular traveling company of stage performers, the Lancashire Lads, knowing its leader to be a Christian gentleman who would watch over him.

It was probably at this time that Charlie, with his devoted brother who was to remain at his side looking after his interests, began to feel the shackles loosen that had bound him from infancy to the Big City at its worst. As he slowly polished his mastery of a career on the stage, the sun that could not penetrate the noxious vapors of the ghetto shed its light on better scenery, and began to brighten his future with promise.

Those bitter-sweet experiences with his harried mother in the slums of London go far to explain his later determination to translate his talents into cash. It required money, and a great deal of it, to break free and to find acceptance in the society of the Big City at its best.

His character remained faulted by scars of childhood, afterward plain to see. As an adult he was not lovable; to many he was not even likeable.

CHAPTER 14: A VIVID AMERICAN CULTURAL SCENE

That his early environment did not bring him to total ruin is something close to a miracle, and for this he could bow in thanks before the sacrifices of his mother Hannah. "Kindness and sympathy were her outstanding virtues," her son tells us, "Not an atom of vulgarity was in her nature," if ever there was one, a God-given blessing.

Ben Turpin did not have any more a countrified upbringing than did Chaplin. Born in New Orleans his family lived there until he was seven, when they moved to New York's lower East Side. His life was uneventful until his late teens when his father put a hundred dollars in his hands and pointed to the door; Ben was kicked out and would be on his own from then on. But he found his way to Jersey City where he foolishly lost his money in a dice game.

To return home was unthinkable, for he was essentially a street person. He hopped a freight for Chicago where he accepted handouts and went door-to-door looking for odd jobs for a few coins. He was not to be found, however, on street corners with a cardboard sign, "Will work for food."

For into his spare frame was built uncommon courage and the unsinkable optimism that proved his salvation from circumstances that brought many a man, and not a few women, to despair. Chaplin and Turpin were equally products of the big city, but the difference between them was as night is to day. His own bitter experiences did not embitter Turpin, and if he had been invited to Fremont to dedicate a motion picture museum he would have accepted graciously and given the event his best effort.

All the others from the Niles studio are forgotten names now, men and women who made their contribution to the profession and like phantoms faded away. Nor did any wax wealthy.

There was Harry Todd, pretty daring as a horseman, according to Jim Wilson who as a youngster bore witness to his risky riding. He relates that Todd was able to conjure up a wild look in his eye and was convincing as "Mustang Pete" before a camera. And there were Billy Reeves, Frank Church and Chester Conklin. Frank Lloyd, in later years famed as a director, could look back to Fremont and Essanay for his early opportunities, as could the skinny ex-window washer Vic Potel. More recently, Virginia

Swanson smiled as she reminisced about slapstick comedienne Sophie Clutts, built like a potato. True Boardman was everybody's favorite, and there was the lovely Joy Lewis, leading lady in the Broncho Billies.

Like an obituary, the list goes on.

15

Trouble Brews as Niles Becomes a Boomtown

Competition among the filmmakers was never far from cutthroat, and it worsened after 1915 as the studios in the LA area gathered speed. William S. Hart, a name not faded entirely even now, was up to his ears in feature films of four and five reels to appease public demand. These longer pictures were being so avidly absorbed that the Broncho Billy two-reelers were becoming obsolete. Anderson was alert to this threat and on numerous occasions tried to impress his partner that Essanay must adapt to the changing times, or else. The alternative was oblivion.

All this was critical, having everything to do with the survival of Essanay. Hairline cracks began to appear in the foundation with reports of loud quarreling in the front office between George and Billy. Much of this had to be over the matter of film length. Spoor was adamant, with his eye on the here and now, insisting that the company was doing well with its shorter pictures, with facts and figures to prove it. Anderson, with an eye to the not-too-distant future, argued that if he was not allowed to expand his Westerns into features the competition would capture the entire market. It must have seemed to Billy that he was no longer dealing with the George Spoor he knew, but with the spirit of old Colonel Selig.

It was during those altercations that Chaplin produced a new feature of his own at the LA studio, his *Burlesque on Carmen*. It seemed to George Spoor that his close attention to that film would be a fair test of Anderson's idea. Off to the theaters went *Burlesque*, and back to his desk came the result in dollars. Disappointed in this, Spoor harrumphed that that was the end of the matter—no features.

Instead of checking out Chaplin, the senior partner would have done better to look at William Hart's work; apparently that did not occur to him.

It was at that time, with Chaplin's contract about to come up for renewal, that Mutual enticed the star away in the same manner that Essanay acquired him in the first place, at a salary ten times higher than he had been receiving. Anderson was of a mind to match Mutual's offer and keep the actor with Essanay, but Spoor behaved as though he'd lost touch with financial reality. Chaplin thus slipped through their fingers, a truly unnecessary mistake and a major setback for Essanay coming at a time when even the older, more established studios were disappearing with a poof. These were no longer the easier days of even five years earlier. Survival of the shrewdest was introducing Darwinian principles into the company boardrooms.

With hindsight we can say that Spoor was demonstrating his ultimate unfitness for his corporation's highest office. Anderson knew this and predicted disaster, seeing nothing but trouble coming down the track. But he was left to stew in his frustrations in the manner of the prophets of old.

The town itself knew nothing of the trouble upstairs. Essanay's tenure of the Fremont lot in Niles was stretching into years, and romance between the studio and the town, a bit bumpy in spots, was blossoming into a marriage. "Niles is forging right ahead," crowed the *Washington Press*, February 21, 1914:

> *The past year's building operations have been the largest for several years…An entirely new class of business buildings is coming in, and when once the town is incorporated and the streets and sidewalks made modern, Niles will rapidly assume the proportions of a little city.*

Witnesses to this saw the new Silva building on First Street and McRae's Theater with two modern stores. The Belvoir was being remodeled, and there was the brand new Ellsworth Packing House. The Senate Restaurant was ready to open, and more construction was planned. This was, in part, the "solution" to the town's "problems" promised by Broncho Billy back in 1912.

CHAPTER 15: TROUBLE BREWS AS NILES BECOMES A BOOMTOWN

And at the bottom of it all was the Bay Area's giant, the Essanay studio, a center of economic well-being that influenced everything it touched. The studio and its outworks represented "…an investment which would probably equal the value of the entire business block of Niles of eight years ago," reported the same issue of the *Press*. Significantly, it added: "Niles has just about doubled its population in the last eight years…" and spoke of the "…gradual strengthening of the local financial situation. The past year has been almost devoid of the financial strain of the previous five years."

If we turn the pages of the paper, we'll see that everything that happened on the movie lot was deemed newsworthy, even when it wasn't. A new feature, *Essanay Notes*, was added to its columns featuring movie micro-news. In March of 1914 one finds the first mention of the Essanay Indians baseball team, then in its third consecutive win of the season.

This team was one of Anderson's ideas which he assiduously watered and pruned as a living advertisement for the studio. He scouted the Bay Area for players and selected them with the same care that he gave to his films. The team was by no means just for recreation, and it could not fulfill his purpose unless it was a winner. And it appears from the papers that the team rarely lost a game. Little wonder, with Anderson glowering at it from the benches.

The movies were honored with lavish coverage with as many as twenty films listed for the coming week. The Saturday matinee at the Bell Theater on May 23, 1914, featured *The End of the Circle* to critical acclaim:

> *One of the best western pictures ever produced. A powerful, gripping story in two great reels, done in genuine Essanay style and produced at Niles. Don't miss this one.*

In another issue, after giving the current Vitagraphs and Kalems and Edisons, one may read a rather quaint article, *Making Hay with Modern Machinery,* "Come in and see everything from cutting the hay to shipping it in bundles." The town, like the nation, was in transition to an industrial base, but for another generation, our agricultural roots would be plain to see.

Niles was squirming to break out of its cocoon toward political maturity. And the surrounding cities were not above a spirit of jealousy. The chamber of commerce at neighboring Hayward paid Essanay the ultimate compliment by attempting to steal it. The details are now lost, but it is certain that overtures were made to Anderson with a view to his breaking camp and relocating over there. The Niles Chamber of Commerce, however, alert for rustlers, headed them off at the pass and the disturbance subsided.

On July 20, 1915, the evolution of the town proceeded at the same pace as the business community debating ways and means of attracting new industry. A committee was appointed to visit the offices of an automobile factory to argue the case for Niles as a splendid location.

The town had been showing healthy vital signs for years and was well on its way to becoming, by now in tight competition with Los Angeles, the center for the motion picture industry in America. The heavily populated East was simply no place anymore for the studios. Increasingly, they were either relocating in the West or withering. Indeed by 1917, and beyond the time frame of our story, Essanay, minus Broncho Billy and with its own days numbered, was one of only two pioneer companies still active.

16

That's Show Biz

The demise of the movie studio in Fremont, with virtually all that the town held dear, came with surprising swiftness. So unexpected was it and so uninformed was the community that there was no mention of Essanay's ailing health at an important citizens' meeting on February 16, 1916.

That was just nine days before the event. Movies were still being turned out at the usual rate, and on the surface, there were no giveaway symptoms of change.

The meeting that Tuesday bustled with an active agenda. And the agenda itself outlined the most ambitious scheme ever raised within the town limits.

By 1916, Niles was close to term; Fremont's heartbeat was audible. On February 4 the *Oakland Tribune* observed, "Niles Has Eye on County Division." Editors of the *Trib* had been keeping a weather eye on things, "Would Incorporate and Await Future Political Developments." The article that followed was a picture of Oakland, the Big City, bemused at the high pretensions of this rustic community:

> With the object of making Niles the seat of government in this portion of the county, a mass meeting of the citizens has been called for next Tuesday night to take the initial steps in incorporating the city. Definite action will be authorized in case a majority of the people are in favor of it. Niles' ambition to become the county center in that section follows the launching in Oakland of the project to establish a consolidated county and city government in the western portion of

Alameda County... Those favoring incorporation argue that Niles, with a population of approximately 1,000, would benefit from the plan and would be in a better position to conduct a county seat campaign.

From the standpoint of sanitation alone, they pointed out, it would be advantageous to incorporate so that an adequate sewer system and other needed utilities could be acquired.

Taking this at face value, we have here a town not even in possession of decent sewage disposal aspiring to leadership in an important county. And with the information then available to the town fathers, the ambition was justified. With this, Niles had arrived at the highest political and economic pinnacle it was ever to experience.

February, 16, 1916, dawned bright and clear. It would be a good day for filming. The crews loaded their cameras and worked through the morning. After taking their usual lunch break, they decided to shoot a few more scenes while the afternoon sun was still high. The name of the picture is unknown, for it never made it to the theaters. While still in mid-picture, a telegram arrived from the home office in Chicago, and the show was over. They packed up their gear, went back to the studio, then to their living quarters to pack their suitcases.

To this day nobody knows the contents of that telegram, but immediately upon receiving it the entire Essanay crew broke camp and pulled out.

The following morning was likewise bright and clear, but there would be no scenes filmed that day, nor ever again. The townspeople awoke to find themselves bereft of their one claim to a grand future. Niles was stunned by a stillness that she hadn't known for years. Deeply affected by this unpredictable turn, her mind was filled with questions that have never been fully answered.

She awoke to find him and his shiny auto gone, and he didn't even leave a note. What is there to say? That's show biz.

· · · · ·

Some sort of inquest is in order, for the breakup of the Fremont studio was a major happening not just for the town and its defeated aspirations, but for the whole of Northern California and the motion picture industry.

And with the demise of this major competitor, Hollywood was more than willing to take up the slack.

By itself, whatever friction there was between Spoor and Anderson cannot explain the death of such a moneymaker even though Anderson did threaten, as reported, to sell out his interest if his partner continued to resist feature-length Westerns. Growing competition with Hollywood was a real menace, and Spoor's tunnel vision surely limited Essanay to a dwindling income from short films. But he was in a position to overrule the tremendous potential of Broncho Billy's Western branch, and that he did.

We may take it deeper.

While the industry down in Los Angeles was still working out of backlots in the sparsely-settled suburbs, Essanay had grown prosperous and formidable under its protective umbrella, the *Motion Picture Patents Company*. Let us recall that it was close to the port cities of Oakland and San Francisco, in an enviable position on a railroad line, with an isolated and lightly-forested valley with rugged terrain close at hand. There was a nearby population pool of movie star wannabes, and seemingly every reason for the studio to remain where it was. The town was in love with it, willing to compromise its conservative ways in return for its manifold blessings. Its economy had been going just swimmingly since the goddess of fortune smiled in 1912, but then like so many other movie enterprises it just evaporated.

In a 1958 interview, George Spoor gave a fragment of an explanation, "Production was discontinued (in Niles) because our facilities were needed for a new type of motion picture called 'Natural Vision.'" The kernel of truth in this piece of fiction is that the Chicago studio was in fact working on a three-dimensional camera, which failed. But the question arises, so what? The new style of camera could have found a lot to do in the wide-open spaces around Fremont.

More to the point is the Supreme Court decision of October, 1915. This had the effect of dissolving the house of cards known as the *Patents Company* by application of the Sherman Antitrust law. The trust-busters in Washington had trained their big guns on their target with effect. And with that, the "Independents" finally savored success in their long struggle upward through the courts.

The once-powerful and hated trust was thereafter broken up into its component parts to be chewed up by the studios that had long been drooling for revenge. This included some of the firms trying to get a start in Los Angeles who now found Essanay, Vitagraph, Lubin and the others naked and within their striking power.

As we have observed, although Spoor had at one time shared Anderson's vision, he had grown brittle and contentious. Ultimately Anderson with his progressive ideas was shelved. He had to sit and watch while William S. Hart carved out the great career that Broncho Billy had marked for his own. After 1916, Hart could breathe more easily, with no fear of competition from the only studio that might have locked horns with him.

A further result was that, just as Essanay had abruptly pulled out of Niles, so did Broncho Billy abruptly pull out of Essanay. And with that, the company was bereft of its guiding spirit. Lessons had come to Spoor too late to be instructive. It was his bad judgment that had brought about the sacrifice of Chaplin, Essanay's biggest financjial attraction. What was it that Lauren Bacall had said? "It's only about money."

Now, with the resignation of Anderson, Spoor had proved to the business world that he had learned nothing with the years. The "A" had departed from the "S&A" logo and that which remained, to use Theodore Roosevelt's apt expression upon leaving the White House in 1909, clung to the fringes of departing glory for a few years longer only to succumb to the inevitable.

Billy's later career is quickly told. His final agreement with Spoor, drawn up by his attorneys at Chicago, contained a provision written by the devil himself by which Anderson was forbidden to create his own films for a period of two years. That Spoor insisted upon this clause is a measure of the fear that he entertained of what his rogue partner might do to him as a competitor. Two years is not a long time, it would seem, but events within the industry had been moving at near-blinding speed and that brief period was long enough. By 1918, when the expiration of that clause set him free, Anderson discovered that two years of inactivity was enough to finish him.

CHAPTER 16: THAT'S SHOW BIZ

The last of the Broncho Billies, *The Son of a Gun*, was the kind of feature film that Anderson had been longing to produce, but the star was by then an anachronism; it proved his dying gasp. The man who was the first to die onscreen in 1903 died once more in 1918, again with a blank in his back. Billy had reached the end of the circle.

Critics today maintain that it was a fine production, judged by the standards of its time. But it was not a financial success, and that made all the difference. Audiences had grown cold. In that two-year period their allegiance had been snapped up by other heroes-of-the-moment.

· · · · ·

By 1918, the attention of the country had been transfixed by the horrors of the war in Europe. The life or death of a movie studio was of no consequence. Broncho Billy was history. Anderson, still young at thirty-five, continued on for a while as a producer, turning out potboilers. With H.H. Frazee he bought the Longacre Theater on West Forty-Ninth street in New York, where they financed a few stage plays that didn't amount to anything. The world of entertainment was finding competition with the Great War just too much. Teaming up with Metro, Billy worked with Stan Laurel on some of his early comedies. (Surely you remember Laurel and Oliver Hardy, the most lovable screwball team of the twenties and thirties?)

And then Anderson had some sort of trouble with Louis B. Mayer, with attorney fees that absorbed more of his diminishing fortune.

But by this time, he was burned out anyway. Although in later years Billy became philosophical about it, when he retired from the picture business he was soured on the whole works.

It is easy to sympathize with him. He was convinced that tremendous opportunities had been missed, and he was probably right.

His final page is the trivia we might expect. There were expensive lawsuits against Spoor, but the two had never really been buddies. And then a suit against Paramount in 1943, enriching only the attorneys. He was embittered against Paramount for having belittled him in the picture *Star-Spangled Rhythm* as a has-been, which was perfectly true, but it rankled. For a while he found something to do as an apartment house manager in San Francisco, with a local reputation, it should be said, for always having a room and a meal for actors on the skids.

Billy resurfaced momentarily in a 1958 television appearance during which he was awarded a special Oscar, a belated honor for his early contributions to the screen.

And then there came one more movie appearance in 1965, in which we catch a final, fleeting glimpse of the great Broncho Billy Anderson in a saloon in *The Bounty Killer*, just sitting there as silent as the days of silent films, ending his career in the way it began as an extra.

His final years were spent at Braewood Sanitarium in South Pasadena, where until 1971 he was left with his memories. And his spirit rode off into the sunset at 5:30 a.m. on January 20, all but forgotten, survived by his wife Molly and his daughter Maxine.

We may now pick up the shovel.

17

Curtain Call

Anderson sold the Essanay property in Fremont to the Ellis Street Investment Company. Its next owner, the California Nursery Company, sold it to Jones and Ellsworth, realtors. Eventually, in 1924, the land and its buildings were released for back taxes to Ed Rose, a longtime resident of Niles, who was given these earthly remains for a mere fifteen-hundred dollars, settling with both Spoor and Anderson to clear the title.

For a while Rose toyed with a forlorn hope of reviving the movie industry, but by then the whole idea had grown stale. The Sympho Cinema Syndicate considered putting the studio to use while keeping offices in Oakland, but nothing came of it.

Nor did anything come of Niles' aspiration to incorporate as a county seat, nor even as a city. And nothing came of the new auto factory, nor of any of the grandiose plans for expansion. It is as though the town had for four years lived an artificial existence. But then, suddenly disconnected from its respirator, Niles reverted to its status as a village.

Newspaper and other records after 1915 and through the 1920s are spotty and the picture isn't clear again until the thirties.

In 1933 the studio buildings were leveled and the ground was cleared. In a brief notice of July 27 of that year, the *Town-Register* intoned, "Last Vestiges of Essanay Studio Removed." The movie playing that evening was *Sundown Rider*, but it was showing at a Hayward theater and Buck Jones was the star. There were no movies at Niles.

Among the tail-end vestiges of the once multimillion-dollar enterprise were a couple of horseshoe prints in a cement driveway on First

Street, a faint echo of the roistering Snakeville Boys, and as close to the Graumann's Chinese Theater ritual that Essanay was able to attain. Even this has been lost, covered with another layer of cement.

· · · · ·

It is as fruitless as it is fascinating to speculate on what might have transpired had the motion picture industry remained firmly in Northern California. But let's give in to the fascination of it for whatever tantalizing surprises may be there. A glance southward will tell us something, although one must understand that the Los Angeles area developed for many reasons in addition to its movie industry.

Fremont as Tinseltown? It could have happened. If the Essanay Company had not given up the ghost, it is conceivable that Fremont would have served as a magnet around which such later giants as RKO, MGM, Paramount and other studios would have clustered. In which case San Francisco would have enjoyed much that has instead accrued to Los Angeles, problems included. Disneyland could have found acreage on the Nimitz freeway, somewhere near the Coliseum. Indeed, the entire political and economic balance of the state would bear little resemblance to what it has become, with a ripple effect in the nation from coast to coast; nothing fundamental can happen in California without being felt across the land.

And perched atop this mountain of confusion and profit, like a star on a Christmas tree, would be the unrecognizable village whose green canyon would be credited by the daily tour guides as responsible for it all. Regular classes at the Charlie Chaplin Museum, along with excursions arranged twice weekly by its staff would serve as a model to inspire the few struggling studios that had chosen to locate in Hollywood, wherever that is.

All of which is a best-case scenario along the road almost, but not quite taken. In 1956, the city of Fremont did incorporate, but its focal point was Washington Township, not Niles. Consigned to a kind of widowhood through no fault of her own, Niles, which is to say Fremont, has entered the present by a far different route, whether for good or ill depending on one's point of view. For there are those, young as well as old, who love

CHAPTER 17: CURTAIN CALL

the face of their town even without makeup.

When the camera crews left, the people had no choice but to revert to the quietude of former years. Around 1925 the chamber of commerce published an undated pamphlet entitled *Why You Should Live in Niles*. It mentioned the two hotels and three churches, plus a theater and a bank, even a local newspaper (a big deal in those days). Fittingly for a community feeling rather tired, a full page advertised the Niles Home for the Aged. Several industries were listed. There was a poultry research farm, a garage, a lumber company and a sand and gravel pit (the first in California). And of course, there was the lovely scenery of the canyon.

"Essanay Notes" had disappeared from the newspaper forever, and the Indians ball team left a vacuum in the sports column never refilled. One searches the paper in vain for any mention of motion pictures, any listing of films to be shown. The entertainment side of life had come to an end. This mirrored the heartfelt interest, and disappointment, that the people had once taken in their studio.

In August of 1916, as the Great War was gaining momentum in Europe, a single ad appeared for the Niles Theater: *The Ne'er-Do-Well*, a ten-act play with Kathlyn Williams and Wheeler Oakman, admission fifteen and twenty-five cents. On September 24 appeared *The Social Highwayman*, from the World Film Corporation, one of the Independents filling the void left by Essanay.

As late as June of 1933 *The Register* ran the following: Clyde Beatty starring in *The Big Cage*, the Baer-Schmelling boxing match, Sylvia Sidney and George Raft playing in *Pick-Up*, Mae West in *She Done Him Wrong*, plus Jimmy Durante and Walter Huston in *Hell Below*. But all of these films were being shown in nearby Hayward, with no pictures whatever mentioned for Niles.

Thoughtful souls ruminated on all of this, reflecting that for some obscure reason a terrific experience had once come to town, had overturned everything and then vanished as in a dream. It had seemed to promise everything just short of salvation, but nothing remained but a whimper. The wound took a very long time to heal, and for many years thereafter the town's loss of interest in everything connected with entertainment seemed permanent.

Lodge meetings, church notices and such tame minutiae as the railroad schedule reasserted itself on the front page.

And "Niles Notes," which never once in those years had lost the thread of local gossip, droned on as if nothing had happened:

> *"The Ladies Guild will meet in the parlors of the Congregational Church next Wednesday June 7."*
>
> *"Mrs. E.B. Tyson spent a day last week with Mrs. Zwister in Pleasanton."*
>
> *"Mr. and Mrs. Philip Moore are enjoying their new automobile, a Ford."*
>
> *"Frank Enos went to the city Sunday and returned Monday."*

End

Interviews with Fremont Residents
Conducted in 1977

The author's heartfelt gratitude is extended to these dear old gentlemen and lovely ladies, the elderly residents of the Niles district. This work would have been impossible without the lengthy conversations by which precious bits of information, gleaned from their lively memories, were revealed, cross-checked, and included in these pages. That they were pretty old when interviewed was necessarily the case because only the testimony of those who were alive, even as children and living near the old studio between 1912 and 1916, could have been relevant to this story.

I was interested to learn that they had never been contacted before by any investigator. These interviews were the first they had ever given. The first and the last. In the years from 1977 to the present they have, one by one, disappeared from the stage of history. But the contributions they have made to this slender volume should reflect the same permanence upon their names as their stories have given to the names of actors and actresses here recorded.

Avila, Harry
Bishop, Marie
Berge, Wilhemina
Carey, Norma
Clute, Mary
Cornish, Ellen
Freitas, Carmelita
Hannah, Betty
Hunt, Lila

Lewis, Ellen
Mozetti, Kathy
Prewitt, Wilma
Silva, Amelie
Swanson, Virginia
Wilson, Jim

Interviewed in 1998:
Art Fereira

In addition, the following friends were most helpful:
Fisher, Dr. Robert –... Fremont

Oakes, George – Resident of Hayward; former owner of the *Township-Register*

Sandoval, John – Hayward; historical editor of the *Hayward Daily Review*

Scott, Evelyn – Author, *When Silents Were Golden*, personal letter

Sheehan, Henry – Deputy Registrar of voters, Alameda County

Viereck, Maxine – Secretary, Hayward Chamber of Commerce

Walker, Erline – City Manager's Office, Fremont

Bibliography

Agee, James. *On Film.* Scranton: Hadden Craftsmen, 1950.

Archer, William. *Fortnightly Review.* vol. 87, 1910.

Baker, Joseph Eugene, *Past and Present of Alameda County, California.* Chicago: Clark, 1914.

Balshofer, F.J. and Miller, A.C. *One Reel a Week.* Berkeley: U.C. Press, 1967.

Bardeche and Brasillach. *The History of Motion Pictures.* N.Y.: Norton & Co., 1938.

Blumer, Herbert. *Movies and Conduct.* N.Y.: MacMillan, 1933.

Brands, H.W. *TR: The Last Romantic.* N.Y.: Basic Books, 1997.

Brownlow, Kevin. *The Parade's Gone By.* N.Y.: Alfred Knopf, 1968.

Chaplin, Charles. *My Life in Pictures.* N.Y.: Grosset & Dunlap, 1974.

Chaplin, Charles. *My Autobiography.* N.Y.: Simon and Schuster, 1964.

Collier's Encyclopedia. Crowel-Collier Pub. Co., 1965.

Corneau, Ernest. *The Hall of Fame of Western Film Stars.* N. Quincy, Mass: Christopher Publishing House, 1969.

Coy, Owen D., ed. *Guide to County Archives of California.* Sacramento: California State Printing Office, 1919.

Crowther, Bosley. *The Lion's Share.* N.Y.: Dutton, 1957.

Cummings, A.R. *California Historical Sites and Landmarks*, chapter 3, "The Essanay Studio." Berkeley; typewritten copy; WPA project, Alameda County Library, 1937.

Elish, Dan. *Theodore Roosevelt.* N.Y.: Marshall Cavendish Benchmark, 2008.

Everson, William K. *A Pictorial History of the Western Film.* Secaucus, N.J.: Citadel Press, 1969.

Everson, William K. *The Hollywood Western*. N.Y.: Citadel Press, 1992.

Faulkner, Harold Underwood. *American Economic History*. N.Y.: Harper & Bros., 1949.

Fell, John. *Film and the Narrative Tradition*. Norman, Okla.: Univ. of Okla. Press, 1974.

Fenin, George N. and Everson, Wm. K. *The Western*. N.Y.: Bonanza Press, 1962.

Fulton, A.R. *Motion Pictures*. Norman, Okla.: University Press, 1960.

Griffith, Richard and Mayer, Arthur. *The Movies*. N.Y.: Simon & Schuster, 1970.

Hampton, Benjamin B. *History of the American Film Industry*. N.Y.: Dover, 1970.

Harbutt, Fraser. *Morgan: American Financier*. Book review, History Book Club. Summer, 1999.

Huettig, Mae D. *Economic Control of the Motion Picture Industry*. Phila.: Univ. of Penna., 1944.

Huff, Theodore. *Charlie Chaplin*. N.Y.: Schuman, 1951.

Hyams, Jay. *The Life and Times of the Western Movie*. N.Y.: Gallery Books, 1983.

Jackson-Wrigley, M. and Leyland, Eric. *The Cinema*. London: Grafton, 1939.

Jacobs, Lewis. *The Emergence of Film Art*. N.Y.: Hopkinson & Blake, 1969.

Jacobs, Lewis. *The Rise of the American Film*. N.Y.: Teachers College, 1967.

Jones, Mark M. *Alameda County: Where Industrial Opportunity Offers a Challenge to Creative Genius*. Oakland: no pub., c. 1915.

Kardish, Lawrence. *Reel Plastic Magic*. Boston: Little, Brown & Co., 1972.

Karney, Robyn, ed. *Chronicle of the Cinema*. London: Dorling Kindersley, Ltd., 1997.

Knight, Arthur. *The Liveliest Art*. N.Y.: MacMillan, 1957.

Kyne, Peter B. *Autobiography*. no pub., 1919.

Lynn, Kenneth S. *Charlie Chaplin and His Times*. N.Y.: Simon & Schuster, 1997.

MacDonald, Gerald; Conway, Michael; and Ricci, Mark. *The Films of Charlie Chaplin*. Secaucus, N.J.: Citadel, 1965

Mast, Gerald. *A Short History of the Movies*. N.Y.: MacMillan, 1986.

BIBLIOGRAPHY

May, Larry. *Screening Out the Past: The Birth of Mass Culture and the Motion Picture Industry.* N.Y.: Oxford, 1980.

McClure, Arthur, ed. *The Movies: An American Idiom.* Madison: Dickenson Univ. Press, 1971.

McGowan, Kenneth. *Behind the Screen. N.Y.:* Delacorte Press, 1965.

Miller, Nathan. *Theodore Roosevelt: A Life.* N.Y.: William Morrow & Co., 1992.

Montgomery, John. *Comedy Films 1894-1954.* London: Allen & Unwin, 1954.

O'Leary, Liam. *The Silent Cinema.* N.Y.: Dutton, 1965.

Parkinson and Jeavons. *A Pictorial History of the Westerns.* N.Y.: Hamlyn, 1972.

Robinson, David. *The History of World Cinema.* N.Y.: Stein & Day, 1973.

Robinson, David. *The Great Funnies.* Suffolk, England: Chaucer Press, 1969.

Robson, E.W. and Robson, M.M. *The Film Answers Back.* London: John Lane, 1947.

Rocq, Margaret M. *California Local History.* Stanford, Calif.: Stanford Univ. Press, 1970.

Sklar, Robert. *Film: An International History of the Medium.* N.Y.: Harry N. Abrams, pub., n.d.

Totha, Paul. *The Filming of the West.* London: Percy Lund, 1960.

Seabury, W.M. *The Public and the Motion Picture Industry.* N.Y.: MacMillan, 1926.

Tuska, John. *The Filming of the West.* N.Y.: Doubleday, 1976.

Wagenknecht, Edward. *The Movies in the Age of Innocence.* Norman, Okla.: Univ. of Oklahoma Press, 1962.

Wenden, D.J. *The Birth of the Movies.* N.Y.: Dutton, 1974.

Wright, Basil. *The Long View.* N.Y.: Alfred Knopf,

www.ingramcontent.com/pod-product-compliance
Lightning Source LLC
Chambersburg PA
CBHW070204100426
42743CB00013B/3045